Tom Bennardo knows mi he has
earned his wisdom one da uide in
the noble cause of church

John O hurch

If you're about to embark on planting a church or becoming a member of a church plant team, you should definitely read *The Honest Guide to Church Planting*. Tom Bennardo tells the truth about the adventure of church planting and will better prepare you for what's ahead.

Dave Ferguson, lead pastor of Community
Christian Church, lead visionary of
NewThing, and author of *Hero Maker*

In *The Honest Guide to Church Planting*, Tom Bennardo is relentlessly open and candid about the very real obstacles that come with planting a church. This book challenges you to view church planting in a more realistic and reliant way that will help your church plant succeed where most fail. Best part? Tom's really quite accurate.

Carey Nieuwhof, founding pastor of Connexus
Church and author of *Didn't See It Coming*

Mission was never meant to be easy, nor has true mission work ever been a cakewalk. Many planters sign on the dotted line, believing all the promises of valor and glory made by the army recruiter, only to find themselves peeling potatoes in the mess hall, wondering what happened. *The Honest Guide to Church Planting* is a timely addition to the turn in conversation that church planting is taking—away from the bright lights and into the real, simple, honest truths that planters need to hear.

Peyton Jones, church planting trainer, podcaster,
and author of *Reaching the Unreached*

As balm is to the wounded, smelling salts to the faint, and a reality check to the delusional—that is what *The Honest Guide to Church Planting* is to church planters. With exceptional insight, naked honesty, and disarming wit, Tom Bennardo probes the inner struggles and outward pressures that church planters face. If you are a church planter, read it. If you are not a church planter, read it and then give it to a church planter.

Craig Ott, professor of mission and intercultural
studies at Trinity Evangelical Divinity School

There's nothing wrong with having a God-given vision, but there's something very wrong about assuming the vision insulates us from difficulties, detours, and pruning. Tom Bennardo gives a painfully honest analysis of the struggles he and many other church planters endure, but his realism isn't a downer. Instead, he points us to Jesus, whose path always leads into suffering, sacrifice, exposure of our motives, and the long process of growth—at least in ourselves and perhaps in our churches. Every chapter is full of wisdom and challenges to our faulty thinking—the kind of insights we desperately need if we have any thought of planting a church.

Dino Rizzo, cofounder and executive director of
the Association of Related Churches (ARC)

Pain and *exhaustion* are better words to describe church planting than *revival* and *Acts 4 community*. Tom Bennardo is willing to admit this truth and provides the wisdom planters need to cultivate correct expectations before finding out the hard way. Jesus gives his church the promise of God's presence, not of being the next greatest movement for our cities. The sooner we can learn from Tom's honest book, the better church planters we will be.

Nick Nye, board member of Sojourn Network and lead
pastor of Apostles Downtown Church, New York City

THE HONEST GUIDE TO CHURCH PLANTING

THE HONEST GUIDE TO CHURCH PLANTING

What No One Ever Tells You about Planting and Leading a New Church

Tom Bennardo

ZONDERVAN
REFLECTIVE

ZONDERVAN REFLECTIVE

The Honest Guide to Church Planting
Copyright © 2019 by Thomas M. Bennardo

ISBN 978-0-310-10099-7 (softcover)

ISBN 978-0-310-10100-0 (ebook)

ISBN 978-0-310-10101-7 (audio)

Requests for information should be addressed to:
Zondervan, *3900 Sparks Dr. SE, Grand Rapids, Michigan 49546*

Cover design: Fort Ventures
Cover photo: Michal Chmurski / Shutterstock
Interior design: Kait Lamphere

Printed in the United States of America

HB 01.05.2022

To Marcia—
my wife, my partner, my lover, and my friend.
On earth there could not be a more vivid picture
of God's beauty and grace.

CONTENTS

FOREWORD

This book needs to be read by anyone involved in church planting. Whether you're a church planter, a coach, or someone who oversees a church planting movement, you need to take these pages to heart.

When I first read Tom Bennardo's musings on church planting, I was blown away. I couldn't believe what I held in my hands was a "first draft." It was too well-written. But what caught my attention even more was the brutally honest yet surprisingly hopeful way he dissected and described the realities of church planting.

As one who personally knows the incredible joys, insecurities, crushing defeats, and the all-consuming focus and passion that come with pastoring a fledgling church plant, I can tell you this book is spot-on. It's filled with things I wish someone had told me in my early days at North Coast Church.

I've noticed that most books in the church planting space fall into one of two categories. They either contain a generic, one-size-fits-all checklist of things a church planter needs to do and expect, or they tell the inspiring story of one particular church's success and the formula behind it.

We've got plenty of the first one. And the second, while uplifting, is seldom very helpful for those who serve in a different church in a different context—which is pretty much all of us.

Instead, what you'll find in these pages is something far more helpful—a candid look at the darker sides of church planting that no one likes to talk about, especially at recruiting events and church planting conferences.

Whether you're toiling in the trenches, having a blast, ready to bail out, or considering whether to jump in and give it a shot, you'll find real-life wisdom to help you along the way.

First of all, thanks to Tom's candor and vulnerability, you'll save a boatload of dumb taxes. He's paid more than his share. Let him save you the grief. There's no need to make the same mistakes he (and most church planters) made.

He'll also help lighten the heavy load of unrealistic expectations that most of us are burdened with. Too often we start off convinced that if we do everything right with a pure and passionate heart, great things will happen. But that's not how it works. We don't determine the kingdom role we play or the fruit of our ministry. God does. And when we forget that, bad things happen. If things don't go as hoped, we end up with unfounded shame and guilt. And if things go better than most, we end up puffed up with foolish pride and begin to look down on others.

Finally, you'll learn the importance of taking the long view— and what that looks like. Frankly, we all tend to overestimate what we can do in one year and greatly underestimate what God can do in five. We want to be an avalanche, not a glacier. But avalanches, while powerful and impressive, don't leave much of a lasting impact. It's the slow-moving glacier that carves out a Yosemite.

If you've got an avalanche ministry, don't get too excited. The things you're so pumped up about today may not be so impressive in a few years. And if you've got a glacier-like ministry, don't get discouraged. Keep at it. God may be carving out a Yosemite.

My expectation is that this book will be a great help to the brotherhood of church planters—men and women who have accepted the call to build up and beautify the bride of Christ.

LARRY OSBORNE, *pastor and author,*
North Coast Church, Vista, California

INTRODUCTION

I thought my story was unique. I was wrong.

I preached my first sermon at sixteen years old. It was part of an international youth competition, and I did it on a dare, mostly for kicks.

Almost immediately, waves of positive feedback flooded my way. They said I was a natural; that something special happened when people heard me preach. Next thing I knew, I was winning the competition and receiving invitations to speak at churches all over the Midwest.

Well-meaning people piled on the accolades, using words like *gifted* and *anointed*. As a young Christian just getting serious about my faith, it was flattering to think God would use me like that. It also fed my already ample Italian ego and imprinted on my soul the belief that my spiritual identity and worth were entwined with my skills and performance. By the end of that year, I concluded this was what it meant to be called into ministry, and with that, the entire trajectory of my life changed.

I became something of a ministry golden child, being elected to leadership positions at my Christian college, winning preaching awards in seminary, directing outreach teams, and then being hired as a youth pastor of a megachurch immediately after grad school. By my twenty-fifth birthday, I was newly married, preaching occasionally to a church of more than six thousand people, being invited to consult with youth ministries around the country, and speaking at retreats and conferences as much as my schedule would allow.

I loved it. Through the next eight years, I poured myself into frenzied but fruitful ministry. The more the work flourished, the more it reinforced my conception of how God moves: you go all-in, committing your life to his service, hone your skills, and step out in faith, and then God sweeps in and energizes your efforts to change the world and transform people's lives. There are challenges and obstacles, to be sure, but if you stick with him and faithfully use the gifts he's entrusted to you, you'll see eternity-changing impact.

The ministry thrived, but over time, my excitement was tempered by a growing restlessness. We'd been doing youth work long enough it felt like we could do it with our eyes closed. I also sensed a nudge that my gift mix might be better suited for a lead role. Marcia and I began quietly praying that God would stretch our faith (I had no idea at the time what I was asking for) and show us where those gifts could be more effectively used.

When a fledgling church plant on the West Coast invited me to become their point pastor, we saw it as God's answer. They were poised to make a major impact but needed someone gifted in communication and leadership to steer the ship forward.

This was it. The faith stretch, we concluded, would be moving ourselves and our two-year-old daughter across the country and leaving behind the comfort and security of a corporate-level church. I'd be pioneering, employing my gifts fully, and experiencing the wonder of God working in us and using us in new ways.

We accepted the call, made the move, and rolled up our sleeves. I threw myself headlong into the world of church planting, full of vigor, bold idealism, and excitement to see God do extraordinary things in our "great adventure."

It didn't take long to notice something was different. For the first time in my ministry life, what I touched didn't immediately turn to gold. I employed all the same skills and energy that had always worked in the past, but this time they didn't elicit the same effect. My preaching didn't seem to wow anyone. My leadership acumen was met with polite nods and little follow-through. Our efforts to mobilize people toward outreach gained no traction. The seeker services we produced featured phenomenal musicians (whom we hired), creative elements, and, of course, my presumably spectacular preaching. And people stayed away in droves.

A series of other factors further impeded our plans. The economy turned sour, and core team members began relocating to pursue new employment. Others dropped out, claiming they felt led by God to transition to other ministries. Six months in, we realized what we were experiencing wasn't just a hiccup; it was a trend. Attendance was dwindling rather than growing; the financial support base was drying up; and we were following a downward trajectory that would run us out of money within the year.

I couldn't find any reasonable explanation for what was happening. The people were fantastic. There was no major dissension or conflict. We just weren't getting anywhere. Everything in the manuals indicated we should be seeing solid, steady growth and movement—we simply weren't.

I shifted into evaluation and problem-solving mode. I rethought our approach. I reread the handful of church planting books available at the time. I prayed for God to reveal what was holding things back. I did a spiritual inventory, asking God to expose sin or unbelief in the camp or even in my own life. I redoubled my resolve to work harder.

Nothing changed. I systematically pulled every trick out of my bag—all of which had worked in the past—and one by one saw them make no difference, until, for the first time in my life, the bag was empty.

At the same time, Marcia and I were experiencing what they call "secondary infertility." We'd had no problem becoming pregnant with our first daughter, but for some reason, our attempts to conceive a second child were unsuccessful. Every month we'd try, and wait, and discover it hadn't happened again. Those who walk the heartbreaking road of infertility know that the longer it goes, the more every month feels like its own mini death. Marcia would be a couple days late; we'd get our hopes up; then she'd wake up in the night and return from the bathroom devastated.

Confusion turned to desperation. I took a long spiritual retreat, begging God to show me what I was missing or what he wanted me to learn. I vowed I'd do anything he wanted. I just needed him to tell me what it was.

The response was absolute silence. I'd always heard stories about how, when you get to the very end of your rope, God shows up and catches you. It didn't prove true. I heard nothing. I felt nothing. I swore I wasn't learning any lessons or deepening my trust. My faith wasn't being stretched or strengthened; it was eroding. There were long spans when Marcia's faith was the only thing that kept us going.

As I agonized over the question of what could possibly be the problem, the best explanation I could come up with was that God was punishing me for some reason. He had withdrawn his anointing. He'd put me on the shelf. But he refused to tell me why. Or maybe the deists were right after all: God spins the world into motion but mostly just turns us loose to make our way and figure it out on our own. Either that, or I simply didn't have what it takes.

The day we determined the church wasn't going to survive,

I drove to the local YMCA to work out, yearning for even a small endorphin release to ease the pain. I intended to swim some laps but never made it into the pool. I stood alone in the gang shower, felt the warm water pounding over my bowed shoulders, leaned my hand against the wall . . . and found I couldn't move. I just stood there, motionless, for the next forty-five minutes, paralyzed by a despondence I'd never experienced before. I was a failure, forgotten and abandoned by God. I've never felt more alone.

Three weeks later, just shy of eighteen months after arriving in town to live the great church planting adventure, we closed the doors for the final time.

Now came the small matter of where to go and what to do next. It was amazing how quickly all the contacts and connections I'd cultivated while at the megachurch had dried up. It seemed people hadn't been enamored so much by my great skill and expertise as by my being attached to one of the largest churches in the country. I was far from my roots, the cloud of a failed ministry hanging over my head, and without a single prospect.

A number of weeks of fruitless job searching followed. And then my path crossed with Don Roth, head of a group I'd never heard of—known today as the Fellowship of Evangelical Churches (whom I now proudly represent). After he listened to my story, I was shocked when he asked if I'd be open to partnering with them to plant a new church back in the Midwest.

The last thing I felt qualified to do at that moment was to plant another church, and I said as much. But Don told me they weren't looking for successful men who knew what they were doing; they were looking for broken men who admitted their weakness but were willing to lead out of that weakness. I was still raw and bleeding, but something about those words felt like oxygen to a suffocating man. An ember of hope I'd thought had been extinguished flickered within my soul. A few weeks later, we packed up, moved cross-country again, and set out to do what I now had absolutely zero confidence to do.

Shortly after arriving in Columbus, Ohio, I felt an inexplicable urge to do something I hadn't done before—seek out other church planters. But I had no desire to glean new strategies or swap success stories. I craved a different kind of fraternity I wasn't sure even existed. So I contacted as many local guys who were planting churches as I could find, invited them to go to breakfast together, and immediately got gut-level honest.

Funny thing about abject failure—it can be a powerful liberator. I launched into the ugliness of my experiences, the intense pain and overwhelming sense of inadequacy and failure they produced. I confessed how deeply it affected me, how exposed I felt when things didn't go the way everybody told me they would go, and how I hadn't had anyone around to talk me off the ledge when I ran out of ideas and hope.

I told these complete strangers I had no real idea what I was doing and I didn't care how it looked or what they thought. I was just going to be honest about how tough church planting is, and I wondered if anyone there had ever felt anything similar.

A couple of them looked at me like I'd just sprouted a third arm. Another suggested a book he thought I might find helpful. One said he couldn't really relate because things were going great for him and he was exceeding all his projections.

But something else happened. Other guys began to tell their own stories. Cautiously at first, like a prison door had been left open and they wondered if they'd be shot if they attempted to escape. But they slowly emerged—heartrending confessions of frustration, depression, fear, and disappointment. They talked about how lonely they felt, how there was no one to go to with their doubts and insecurities because they had to be the flag wavers and vision casters to keep everyone else's hopes alive and financial supporters giving. Each new voice said he'd always thought he was the only one.

Perhaps most significantly, the details of their accounts were eerily similar to each other's, and to my own. It confirmed something profoundly significant to me: my experience wasn't unique. All along I'd been neither special nor inadequate nor abandoned. I was typical.

The more these brothers talked, the more another shared perspective emerged: they couldn't understand why no one had warned them what church planting would really be like. Why had they been painted such an unrealistic picture of pioneering? Why had they been conditioned to believe the combination of right planter with right message and right methodology in the right target area would equate to assured outcomes?

No one had ever explained to them that what they were witnessing were universal experiences in church planting. No one had told them the path wouldn't in any way resemble the guys they'd seen featured at the conferences to inspire them. They'd been left to navigate the journey themselves, convinced any disparity was due to their own incapacity to replicate the proven models.

That conversation became the seedbed for some life-saving connections in my own journey that you'll read about later. It also served as the flashpoint for a commitment I've attempted to keep ever since. Extending through my transitions from church planter to sending church pastor, to mentor and encourager of church planters, I've vowed to be a voice that would counter the systematized success-story formulas commonly presented to church planting recruits and those already in the game.

For more than twenty-five years since, I've encountered not only a steady stream of disillusioned and discouraged church planters, but countless casualties—once-enthusiastic planters whose experiences so beat them up they never fully recovered. More of them than I can count closed their churches. Many left ministry permanently. Some abandoned the faith altogether.

If these casualties could have had a credible source assuring them their heartaches and inertia were absolutely common, even among the best of us, they may have experienced a different outcome. Some may have been able to hang in there longer. Perhaps a few would be counted as more than just statistics today.

This is not a how-to book on church planting. It's for those toiling in the trenches, those about to bail out, and those considering jumping in. It's for the brotherhood of church planters laboring and struggling, seeing little movement and wondering what they're doing wrong or why God is failing them. My sincere hope is to spark some candid conversation and provide a source of perspective and honesty for that fraternity. Together we can embrace a much truer, more accurate, more realistic picture of what planting a church is really like—one that may just enable us not only to survive it but to thrive in it.

THE TRUTH ABOUT *YOU*

or

The "Destined for Greatness Thing"

Y ou're not going to like this.

If you've ever felt an inkling to plant a church—even just a passing thought that it might be something you could do—two things are almost certainly true of you: you're passionate about reaching lost people, and you're arrogant.

Don't take offense. Every leader who has ever served God's kingdom has done so with, at best, mixed motives. By its very nature, church planting requires a belief that a new church can accomplish something better than is currently being done, and that you're someone who can do it.

Call your motivation to plant a church whatever you like—entrepreneurship, a pioneering spirit, holy discontent. But somewhere in the mix lies the presumption that you possess a superior way, superior skills, superior drive, or all three. You wouldn't become a church planter if it weren't so.

LEADERSHIP'S EVIL TWIN

Church health and growth researchers almost universally list leadership as the single most essential quality needed to effectively pastor a church. That is especially true for church planters. The ability to capture and articulate a vision for a preferable future, enact a plan to achieve it, and catalyze others to bring it to fruition is crucial for any pioneering role. Analyst George Barna went so far as to say, "I believe nothing is more important for the future of the Christian Church in America than leadership."[1] Given the current state of the church in this country, that's hard to dispute.

Understandably, then, most church planting recruitment and assessment centers prioritize the identification of "high-level leaders." If a man can't lead, he won't be able to plant.

The leadership gift is rare. But if you've aspired to become a church planter, you're probably convinced you possess it. And if others have affirmed your calling to plant a church, they most likely agree.

Therein lies your problem.

Leadership, imperative as it is, is always accompanied by its evil twin—Arrogance. The same gland that produces confidence and charisma also secretes the toxins of pride and self-trust. Gary McIntosh and Samuel Rima call it "the dark side of leadership."[2] Hubris. Ego. Arrogance. The innate belief that one's capacities, knowledge, and skill are superior, even indispensable to the success of the endeavor. The quality most essential to leading an effective church plant carries a perverse contaminant that breeds narcissism.[3] As Gordon Livingstone wrote, "Our greatest strengths also prove to be our greatest weaknesses."[4]

Apricots are one of the world's healthiest fruits. Nutritional heavyweights, they're packed with antioxidants, high in fiber, and brimming with vitamins A and C. They're great for the immune system, blood and bone health, and young-looking skin.

They can also kill you. Apricot pits contain elevated levels of amygdalin, a compound that breaks down into hydrogen cyanide when ingested. Yes, cyanide. Four or five apricot pits, if opened and consumed, can dispatch a 150-pound man in a matter of hours. One fruit, two effects: it can nourish you, and it can take you out.

Leadership and arrogance likewise emanate from the same fruit. They so resemble one another, and so thoroughly intertwine, that it can be impossible to distinguish between them or extricate the latter without also crippling the former.

In my nearly three decades of working in church planting, the most consistent, common trait I see among church planters is deep-seated, pervasive arrogance. Oh, we can preach (better than anyone, mind you) on pride and its insidious effects. We say we're aware of its presence in our lives, and we've taken tangible steps to keep it at bay. But it penetrates far deeper into our hearts than we admit or even comprehend.

THE DESTINED FOR GREATNESS THING

As I described in the introduction, I experienced early success and significant accolades for my preaching and spiritual leadership. The affirmation and recognition so attached themselves to my identity and worth that they became embedded within my personal theology. I believed my value to God was evidenced by his unbroken blessing on my ministry and his anointing on my leadership. I was sure I was intended for extraordinary things.

As I traveled around speaking at evangelistic rallies, I calculated that about the time I'd be hitting my prime, Billy Graham would be reaching retirement age. Connect the dots, and I could see the plan unfolding. I was set apart. Uniquely gifted by God. Special.

I never said it aloud, but I sincerely believed there was no way I would die young. God had too much invested in me and too much planned for me.

They were the thoughts of a narcissist. I'm ashamed now that I even thought them, and of course I never admitted them to anyone. But that didn't change the fact that, at my core, I believed them. The disease, what we now affectionately call the "Destined for Greatness Thing," was there, growing and spreading, driving me to compulsive levels of excellence and big hairy audacious goals, all infused with ministry zeal and camouflaged in dedication.

I recall driving along a lonely stretch of Manchester Road outside Akron, Ohio, pretty much in the middle of nowhere, when I caught a glimpse of a little brick church building. I'd passed it dozens of times and hadn't ever noticed it. This time I did. Near the road stood one of those typical, brick-framed marquee church signs with the interchangeable plastic lettering—the kind where someone spells out cheesy sayings they think are clever but really just embarrass themselves. At the bottom of the sign I noticed the pastor's name, with a letter or two missing and a couple more dangling off-kilter.

I remember thinking how awful it must be to be that guy— limited by his lack of gifting, stuck in a country church no one cared about, trying to convince his smattering of sheep he was worth following. I was certain I was intended for more than a typical church with a nondescript history that struggled along and made little impact. God had chosen me for far better. I was destined for greatness.

Your level of arrogance may not parallel my full-blown narcissism, but if you're a church planter, you carry the same disease.

And God is committed to doing something about it.

THE GREAT WEAKENING

In the sci-fi comedy classic *Men in Black*, Will Smith's character is recruited to become the next clandestine agent protecting earth from alien misconduct. When he agrees, he says to his recruiter, "All right, I'm in . . . But before y'all get to beaming me up, there's just a few things you should know. First off, you chose *me*, so you recognize the skills. And I want nobody calling me 'son' or 'kid' or 'sport' or nothing like that, cool?"

Tommy Lee Jones's veteran agent responds, "Cool, whatever you say, slick. But I need to tell you something about all your skills . . . As of right now, they mean precisely [squat]."[5]

You won't find it in the recruiting pamphlets, but when you step into church planting, job one will not be to develop your team-building gifts, your vision-casting abilities, or your missional-outreach expertise. It will be God's systematic elimination of some of the very skills and stabilities you thought qualified you for the gig. He will commence major surgery . . . on you.

We might call it the Great Weakening.

Part of this we understand. We're well aware of the "when I am weak, then I am strong" principle—how God uses "jars of clay" to accomplish his purposes (2 Corinthians 4:7). We've all quoted A. W. Tozer: "It is doubtful whether God can bless a man greatly until He has hurt him deeply."[6]

What we're not as ready for is the form the Great Weakening takes. We fully expect to be spiritually attacked—and temporarily slowed—by oppositional forces like hard soil, enemies of the gospel, and fleshly temptation. But God employs surgical instruments that cut into the very muscles empowering us to lead in the first place.

I've observed that the Great Weakening generally strikes one or more of four predominant areas of our lives, close to home and central to our character:

1. *Physical/Emotional health*—A debilitating medical condition or disease in ourselves or in someone close to us. Or a surprisingly severe onset of depression.

2. *Marriage and family*—Previously hidden issues or new dynamics that strain marital oneness and trust. Or significant parenting or extended family issues.
3. *Finances*—Unexpected changes that capsize our financial situation. Or evaporating income sources or major expenses that create intense financial pressure and hardship.
4. *Ministry*—Lack of responsiveness, opposition from surprising sources, rapid attrition, or even outright betrayal, which rock the foundation of our efforts. Or previously successful methods and skills that simply stop working.

It's impossible at first to tell the difference between a faith test, an enemy attack, and the first incision of spiritual surgery. Our initial response is usually to ramp up our efforts, pray it through, and invite God to bring victory.

Many of the challenges and setbacks, even some very intense ones, pass in time. But when the scalpel of the Great Weakening falls, the incision is slow, deep, and painful. The surgery doesn't abate. The wound refuses to heal. We lean hard into God but find that no amount of faith, prayer, or obedience brings restoration. Eventually we're struck with the haunting prospect that we're enduring an affliction we did not seek, for a purpose we cannot understand, before a God who will not intervene.

Brennan Manning labeled this the "second call." In his bestseller *The Ragamuffin Gospel*, he suggested it usually presents itself to leaders sometime between the ages of thirty and sixty. "They can no longer keep life in working order," he wrote. "They are dragged away from chosen and cherished patterns to face strange crises. This is their second journey."[7]

I heard Manning speak before he died, and something else he said struck me. "A pastor can minister in the power of the flesh until about his mid-thirties," he said. "After that, because he is so deeply loved, his Abba will begin to surgically remove some of his most precious, God-given provisions. When that happens, he'll accuse God of cruelty. But he is actually receiving one of the most gracious gifts God will ever give him."

GOD'S DEAFENING SILENCE

The surgery sears our souls and threatens to irreversibly damage our self-confidence. Its most painful facet, though, is how God chooses not to intercede, nor even to allow us to sense his presence, in the midst of it. We pray, and we see nothing. We seek God's assurance and presence, but we feel nothing. Like Job, we call out, "I cry out to you, God, but you do not answer; I stand up, but you merely look at me" (Job 30:20). We experience a very real death and begin a slow walk through the stages of grief, moving from denial to anger, to bargaining with God, on to depression—even to despondence.

But the surgery is purposeful. "God's silence is how it feels, it's not how it is," Jon Bloom once wrote.[8] Something is happening; we're simply not capable of recognizing it. It's a severe mercy. Larry Crabb summarized this in *Shattered Dreams*: "God's restraint has a purpose. When He appears to be doing nothing, He is doing something we've not yet learned to value and therefore cannot see. Only in the agony of His absence, both in the real absence of certain blessings and in the felt absence of His Presence, will we relax our determined grasp of our empty selves enough to appreciate His purposes."[9]

The Great Weakening resets the very foundations of our identity and ministry. We're stripped of that which defined us, forced to scrounge for something other than our inherent gifts and resources to validate our worth. While we flounder, we watch as God still accomplishes his purposes, independent of our contribution, unfazed by our impotence. In the course of time, we hear him whisper that his love for us and value of us have continued uninterrupted. We're highly favored, cherished beyond comprehension, and still invited to participate in what he alone is effectuating in our world.

A level of brokenness emerges . . . if we cooperate with it. A deeper kind of humility. We find ourselves craving the spotlight a little less. We understand the "broken and contrite heart" of Psalm 51:17 a little more. We read 2 Corinthians 1 a little differently.

The Great Weakening is inevitable and essential. But there's still more to it.

THE PRINCIPLE OF PERPETUAL WEAKENING

I've come to the place where I can reluctantly accept the weakening process. I see God's wisdom in preserving his rightful glory and purging my self-trust.

But there's a further aspect to his way that I can never quite get used to. It's the revelation that God doesn't weaken his chosen instruments and subsequently reward them with strength. *God keeps them in a state of perpetual weakness.* He continues to introduce further weakening agents into their path for the entirety of their lives.

That's frankly not what we signed up for. Our theology allows for God to refine us with early failure, so long as he later rewards us with victory and power. That's the purpose of resistance training, right? Tear down the muscle so it can rebuild stronger. We've accepted the painful pruning, but we keep waiting for the payoff. We're convinced if we pay enough dues and learn enough humility, God will reward us with at least a measure of the vision we've always embraced. We figure he owes us that much.

We're quick to quote Paul's famous 2 Corinthians 12:10 declaration, "When I am weak, then I am strong," mistaking it to say,

"After I've been sufficiently weakened, God makes me strong." But notice, Paul didn't say his weakness resulted in becoming strong. He said God's strength was manifested *in his state of weakness*. Paul described ongoing weakening as his normative, perpetual condition. In a less-often-quoted section of that same letter, he wrote, "We *always carry around* in our body the death of Jesus, so that the life of Jesus may also be revealed in our body" (2 Corinthians 4:10, italics added).

When Ananias questioned God's methodology—perhaps even his sanity—in selecting Saul the Christian-hunter to become Paul, the preeminent missionary to the Gentile world, God's response was, "I will show him how much he must suffer for my name" (Acts 9:16). The promised suffering would not be retribution for Paul's past atrocities. Those had already been absolved by a super-abounding grace (see Romans 5:20). God was simply disclosing his modus operandi for his chosen leaders. He persistently weakens them.

God does this for good reason. The disease of self is never eradicated this side of heaven; it can be only brought into remission. To discontinue treatment is to risk recurrence. The cancer is prone to return with ferocious vengeance, metastasizing in ways that destroy the carrier. When God maintains treatments that unceasingly weaken his servants, he isn't showing himself to be a sadist; he is mercifully shielding them from their own poisons.

The Great Weakening is therefore not a means to an end; it is a permanent condition. Jacob walked with a limp for the rest of his days. Opposition and failure plagued Moses throughout his life. The prophets spent the majority of their ministries running for their lives and died mostly poor, ineffective, and disliked. Paul was dogged by detractors and subjected to constant discomfort. And, as far as we can see in Scripture, his thorn in the flesh never healed.

The question, then, becomes, can you be okay with that?

EMBRACING OUR CONDITION

One of the hallmarks of Alcoholics Anonymous is a practice where recovering alcoholics consistently self-identify as such. Regardless of how many years of sobriety they may have attained, the traditional in-meeting self-introduction remains the same: "Hi, my name is _____, and I'm an alcoholic." Some have criticized this as stigmatizing, branding oneself with a shaming scarlet letter. But most of the AA veterans I've known wear it as a badge of honor. To them, it reflects an emancipation achieved through honest self-admission.

God's relentless surgery produces a similar reidentification, if we only let it. Those undone by the Great Weakening don't simply resign themselves to its ongoing presence; they also embrace it as a holy gift from a gracious Father. They don't wallow in their weakness, and they don't pretend to enjoy its pain, but they soften into a quiet freedom. They retain the strengths of their leadership gifts but exercise them with increased grace. They develop a deeper, more substantive confidence, one free from the demand that their agendas be fulfilled. They look and interact a lot more like Jesus.

Mike Dittman was one of the most talented pastors I'd ever met. Tall, athletic, and good-looking, he possessed a magnetic personality and skillfully led a college ministry that drew hundreds of believers and seekers alike. He was a fantastic musician and an exceptional basketball player. He was funny and articulate. He loved Christ, was crazy about his wife, and adored his children.

I co-pastored on the same staff with Mike, and we became good friends. He was the kind of guy who should make you insanely envious, except that he was so doggoned likeable and self-deprecating you couldn't help but love him.

Everything changed for Mike one afternoon at the gym when, after a routine workout, he collapsed and became instantly unresponsive. Paramedics were called but were unable to resuscitate him. He was rushed to the hospital where it was determined Mike had lived his first thirty-one years with an undetected, genetic defect in the blood vessels of his brain. He'd never displayed a symptom until an artery suddenly exploded, creating a severe brain hemorrhage. He was rushed into emergency surgery; his wife, Pam, was summoned; and everyone was told to prepare for the worst. It was almost certain that Mike would not live. In a matter of minutes, he went from a gifted spiritual dynamo to a comatose shell on the verge of death.

Miraculously, Mike survived the surgery. But as he recovered, the doctors informed him that the artery in his brain was a ticking time bomb. He could either live with it and know that an almost certainly fatal brain hemorrhage could recur at any time, or he could choose a very risky additional surgery. They informed him that if he survived the surgery, it could solve the problem but would more than likely result in significant, permanent paralysis.

After agonizing prayer and discussion, Mike chose the surgery. It was successful, but sure enough, he lost functionality of most of the left side of his body. His facial muscles would not work, so one side of his face drooped, and his left eye had to be sewn shut because it wouldn't produce sufficient moisture to prevent infection. He couldn't use his left arm. He walked with a noticeable limp. The condition was permanent.

Mike could no longer play basketball or guitar; he was unable to speak without a noticeable impediment; and he couldn't pick up his children. But he survived. And he continued to serve Christ—albeit in a much different capacity.

A few years later, I spoke with Mike about what he'd learned through it all. He talked about how his journey had exposed a self-reliance he hadn't known he'd carried. He confessed how, prior to the stroke, he'd operated with an awareness of his giftedness that validated his worth and fed his pride. He admitted how, even when he'd tried to purge the darker aspects of his ego, they had still flowed through his actions and attitude.

Then he talked about how his misfortune produced an awareness of God's mercy and presence he had never known before. He told how his intimacy with God as his Father had burrowed to depths he couldn't previously fathom. He shared how his impact for God's kingdom now took a radically different shape. He said he'd come to the place where, if he could go back in time and decide to forgo the surgery or even eliminate the disease entirely, he would choose to walk through it all again for the effect it had on his heart and life.

I told him I didn't believe him. That's the kind of thing people say as a coping mechanism when they're trying to spin-doctor their situation to protect God's image or convince themselves they're okay when they're not. But over time, I saw that Mike absolutely meant it. He had become a fundamentally different leader, a different man. He viewed his weakening as a holy gift, and the depth of his impact was forever transformed.

Mike's surgery was literal and extreme. But every leader who aspires to a position of influence for God can expect him to inject substantial, lasting weakening agents into his path.

Few church planters are warned about this part of the journey. Perhaps that's a good thing, because if we were, nobody in their right mind would sign up for it willingly. But you don't choose it. God chooses it for you and supplies a grace capable of remaking you through it.

You may not be able to avoid the Great Weakening, but you can be aware it's coming, and you can respond to it differently when it arrives. Don't be surprised when the knife cuts. Don't view it as your enemy. Don't wallow in doubt and self-loathing after the failures and dream-crushing effects they produce.

And don't abandon ship. Walking through the valley of the

shadow of death molds you into the "wounded healer" Henri Nouwen described, opening a depth of impact you could never have tapped into otherwise. Nouwen wrote, "For a deep understanding of his own pain makes it possible for him to convert his weakness to strength and to offer his own experience as a source of healing to those who are often lost in the darkness of their own misunderstood sufferings."[10]

Let it produce a humility that moves you forward in confidence and trust but always keeps you aware that you're a recovering narcissist.

Over the years, I've had well-meaning people approach me after a Sunday service, saying that what our church had going on was so good, so impactful, that "this thing is going to explode." They were referring to attendance, facilities, and notoriety, of course—the typical ways people measure God's blessing. My response became almost routine. I would thank them politely, and if pressed, I'd say, "God is more than welcome to do that if he chooses, but I kind of doubt he'll ever let it happen. I have a feeling he loves me too much."

You think you're forming a church. God is forming a person.

CHAPTER 2

THE TRUTH ABOUT "PROVEN" METHODS

or

You Can Organize a Church to Death,

but You Can't Organize One to Life

Walk into a church planting conference and you'll see it instantly. The gauntlet.

Endless lines of exhibitor booths and resource tables. Smiling reps in matching, logo-embossed polo shirts ready to demonstrate how combining your skills and zeal for church planting with their field-tested, can't-miss strategies and resources will exponentially increase your probability of success.

It's one-stop shopping. Everything you need right there at your fingertips—signage and banners for promotion, built-to-spec carts fitted with all the necessary equipment, top-shelf curriculum for the mandatory killer children's ministry. Discipleship tools, movie theatre deals, plug-and-play webcasts of your services . . .

And, of course, there is "The Plan." A guaranteed, surefire model for effective and successful church planting.

Perhaps that's an overstatement. But as evidence, let me offer these actual quotes from church planting network websites:

- (Our) model has been proven through the launch of hundreds of churches, with large launch day attendance and long-term success that exceeds national averages. When you choose to launch with (us), you have access to all the resources that make this possible.
- We help you succeed through our seven proven systems created by leaders across the country to improve the success rate and effectiveness of church planting.
- Our model is designed to provide an operating system—a done-for-you, integrated framework based on proven church planting and leadership principles—to assess and train your church planters to launch healthy churches.

Church planting has evolved into a cottage industry, rising from relative obscurity three decades ago to form its own ecosystem. The inevitable science has followed, as denominations and networks have studied and quantified what works and what doesn't. The result is an array of refined, clearly demarcated, easy-to-understand plans for launching a thriving church. Like cellular phone companies, they all boast of superior network reliability and higher customer satisfaction.

There's little reason to doubt the claims. They're flush with money and testimonials; their materials are slick; and they seem genuinely impassioned to reach the lost and establish reproducing churches. Plus, they report unheard-of success rates.

THE HIDDEN CASUALTIES

Now follow me into the real world. Your world, if you're a church planter.

Trevor is a gifted, passionate leader. He's served effectively as a staff pastor in a healthy, established church. As he seeks God's direction for his future ministry, he feels the undeniable pull to step out by faith with a dream to launch a new church. He works with his current church and targets a neighboring community ripe for transformational, incarnational, missional outreach.

He readily admits he's no expert, but he's motivated and eager to learn. After prayerfully evaluating the options, he partners with a church planting network and adopts a method perfectly matching his own ideas and instincts. He sails through the assessment process, thrives in the training, and ventures out with a truckload of hopes, meticulously following the prescribed game plan.

Somewhere along the way—perhaps six months in, perhaps a year—he feels the first rumble of uneven road beneath his wheels. The fund-raising isn't matching the projections. The core team isn't growing at the rate the charts indicated. The launch service falls noticeably short of the projected attendance. The first-class marketing piece produces disappointing returns.

And then there's the people. Some he thought he could count on suddenly drop out. A key leader moves out of the area. Another feels God calling her back to the mother church. Complaints start finding their way back to him, from those who should know better than to grumble to others instead of coming directly to him first (we'll talk more about this in chapter 4).

At first, Trevor scratches his head and figures things will come around. He does some systems checking and tweaking. He heightens his resolve. He attends a conference to recharge his batteries.

But the condition lingers. Now the results are falling noticeably behind the projection charts. He convenes his core people to re-envision them toward higher commitment. He has a frank talk with his coach, who offers some solace, tips, and encouragement, but is himself a bit perplexed.

Still the trend continues. Attendance not only doesn't increase; it declines. The funding clock continues to tick, but more significantly, Trevor begins a quiet slide toward self-doubt, discouragement, and fear. He privately begins to wonder if he misheard God's call. He's worried, but he can't reveal his growing uncertainty publicly—a solid group of sincere, Jesus-loving people are counting on him, trusting him, looking to him for answers and hope. He musters up the energy to keep the vision alive. But every month, it drains a bit more, until he finds himself at a crossroads.

After trying everything he knows—regrouping, recommitting, relaunching—Trevor makes the painful decision to close the effort down. He limps from the wreckage with more questions than answers, his dreams shattered and his self-esteem quashed.

This story, in a myriad of variations, has repeated itself countless times across the country. And it represents the first of the church planting industry's dirty little secrets: the roadside is strewn with casualties.

"THREE KINDS OF LIES: LIES, DAMNED LIES, AND STATISTICS"

You'll see some lofty statistics published by church planting organizations. I've read success rate claims as high as 100 percent. But far more church planting endeavors close in their first five years than are reported by denominations or networks.

There's wide disparity over the actual failure rate. Some estimate it to be close to 35 percent, some closer to 50/50, and others suggest it reaches as high as 80 or even 90 percent. I suspect many who boast of improbably high success rates employ some "creative" statistical methods to land there, while those with dismal track records are reluctant to publish hard numbers at all. My own estimate, based on actual projects I've personally observed, is that between one-half and two-thirds of church plants fold their tents within their first decade.

But the casualty list isn't limited to failed churches. It extends to the church planter himself, who sees it happen on his watch. When the beta-tested, all-but-guaranteed plan proves unsuccessful, the only explanation left to the planter is that *he* is the reason for the failure. Unless someone or something intervenes to convince him otherwise, the long-term effects may prove devastating.

I've personally witnessed too many good men who have closed their church plants permanently scarred. One whom I consider a personal friend was left so reeling from his failed plant, he began exploring alternative philosophies and ideologies from thinkers like Christopher Hitchens and Richard Dawkins, considering theories that perhaps the "God delusion" was behind everything he'd built his worldview around. Today he would call himself an atheistic humanist.

Stories like these aren't statistics on a page. They're living, breathing souls, staggered by a disillusionment they weren't prepared to face.

To lay blame for these casualties solely at the feet of the church planting industry would be grossly unfair. But one unintentional side effect of presenting methods and resources as "proven successful" is the presumption that standardized systems produce assured outcomes.

Where did that thinking come from?

HOW METHOD BECAME KING

Much of this rationale can be traced to the rise of what is now called predictive retail science. The technological advances of the late 1900s allowed the United States retail industry to study shoppers' habits in ways they never could before.

American consumers, it was quickly discovered, follow very predictable patterns. When entering a store, they immediately turn to the right and follow a counterclockwise path.[1] They don't notice signage or products placed within the first fifteen feet of the entrance. They walk to the right and reach to the right. They speed up at banks and slow down at reflective surfaces.[2] (I can confirm this . . . my wife has always said I can't pass a mirror without stopping to look at myself in it.)

Seems we're more like cattle than we'd like to think, easily herded and entirely predictable.

But it doesn't stop there. It turns out consumer behavior can be not only predicted but directed. By manipulating sight lines, product placement, and traffic flow, merchants can all but guarantee what we will see, what we will buy, and how much we will spend. One study showed 60 percent of what we purchase once we're in the store wasn't on our list when we arrived.[3]

Modern masters of the process, like Amazon and Apple, have so perfected predictive analytics that they've developed models remarkably effective at capturing our attention, convincing us of a need, and steering us toward a predetermined decision. Environmental psychologist Paco Underhill likens it to a spiritual experience. "The Apple store is not a store," he said, "It is an exercise in evangelism."[4]

It's no shock that as the church planting industry grew, similar analytical tools were employed to determine and develop consistently effective methodologies. Call it the science of church planting: gather a preponderance of data, track recurrent patterns, isolate best practices, consolidate them into a reproducible system, and package it as a proven method that, if implemented precisely, will produce consistent, predictable results.

Except it doesn't.

And there's a reason.

THE ONLY CONSTANT IS CHANGE

Lost in the systematizing of church planting methodology lies a fundamental distinction: the church isn't an industry, and spiritual transformation can't be mass-produced.

At least four different factors guarantee church planting will defy standardization:

1. **The myth of "experts."** James Altucher, a renowned hedge fund manager and venture capitalist, was asked how he became an expert at predicting business trends. He replied, "There is no such thing as an expert."[5] Rather, he said, there are only those with experience, education, and resources, and they still regularly fail miserably at predicting future outcomes. Altucher, who is considered one of the most successful entrepreneurs of his era, has noted that of the twenty-plus companies he founded or cofounded, more than seventeen had folded.

The most studied, brilliant analysts still routinely flop at producing long-term, consistent models of success. It holds true across practically every discipline—medicine, real estate, politics, business, entertainment.

The motion picture industry retains an army of market research firms and experts and is regularly perplexed when a *Napoleon Dynamite* becomes a box office hit while a *47 Ronin* loses nearly $150 million. No expert model could have accurately predicted *Gengham Style* would go viral, "the Snuggie" would move 30 million glorified towels, or Donald Trump could be elected president. Those who claim to be experts are usually selling something.

2. **The church isn't a business; it's a living organism.** To be sure, the church operates as an organization and possesses many of the same characteristics as a business. But at a cellular level, it exists as a fundamentally different creature. The church is first and foremost a spiritual entity and a living organism. Scripture

calls it a "body." Comprised of biotic beings, it is complex and unpredictable, full of organic frailties and susceptible to disease. Its foundational components are not brick and mortar, machines and widgets, but thinking, breathing, volitional people who make wildly erratic choices based on whim, individual priorities, and selfishness. Any enterprise trading in human volition can never be standardized.

3. **The very real subversions of a very real enemy.** The church planter's primary objective is to invade enemy territory and reclaim it for a rival King. You're warring against the combined forces of a sworn enemy diametrically opposed to your cause, armed with millennia' worth of guile and craft to subvert your efforts.

Jesus warned that if you want to plunder someone's possessions, you must first tie up the strong man (Mark 3:27). The god of this world isn't relinquishing his hard-won territory without a fight. You can expect countermeasures, surprise attacks, and the dirtiest of tactics to be employed. You don't waltz into the enemy's camp and expect to raise the rival's flag. As Boromir declared to the Council of Elrond in *The Lord of the Rings*, "One does not simply walk into Mordor."[6] Mike Tyson famously said, "Everybody has a plan until they get hit."[7] Someone packing a far harder punch is awaiting your "plan."

4. **The most significant factor: God defies predictability and sabotages attempts to systematize his ways.** The heroine in C. S. Lewis's *Chronicles of Narnia*, Lucy, asks the Christ figure, Aslan, why he didn't come roaring in to rescue them "like last time." Aslan replies, "It is hard for you, little one . . . But things never happen the same way twice."[8] When you serve the Most High God, you're operating on behalf of one who refuses to be reduced to repeating methods or prescribed timetables. He almost never does the same thing the same way twice.

Look at the pattern-defying military strategies God employed with Israel's armies. On one occasion, he tells them to cross a miraculously parted sea that collapses behind them to drown the enemy. On another, he commands them to march seven times around a walled city and then shout, disintegrating the walls. On still another, he instructs them to send the celebrants to the front lines as if the battle is already won, and then he confuses the enemy armies to turn and annihilate each other. Every now and then, he even orders the Israelites to pick up weapons and actually fight.

Think about the methods Jesus used to heal. This time, he's spitting on dirt and rubbing it on a man's eyes. Next time, he's commanding diseased people to report to the priest. Another time, he's sticking his fingers in someone's ears. He's touching some, speaking to some, and simply telling others to go home and find their loved ones healed.

Why the lack of repeated patterns?

THE INSOLUBLE GOD

The Bible never gives a definitive reason, but it's certainly logical to assume that God refuses to be reduced to formulas, manipulations, or predictability. He goes to great lengths to ensure his movement is seen exclusively as *his* movement, not the result of our ability to solve him or systematize his ways.

The wind of God's Spirit, Jesus said, blows where it pleases (John 3:8). You don't manufacture wind. You don't dictate the direction it must blow. You simply raise your sails and harness its power.

Not only does God seldom repeat his methods, but he doesn't take kindly to presumptions that he will. Exodus 17 records God's provision of water for the parched, wilderness-wandering Israelite refugees. He instructs Moses to perform the unorthodox faith act of striking a boulder with his staff. Moses obeys, and a river miraculously gushes from the rock.

When the nation later finds itself in a similar situation—the people clamoring as if they've completely forgotten the whole water-from-a-rock thing—God intervenes again. This time he switches up the plan and tells Moses to speak to a rock (Numbers 20:8).

Speaking to a rock shouldn't seem any more ridiculous a water-tapping method than whacking one. But for reasons the Scripture doesn't elaborate on, Moses disregards the new instruction and repeats the method that worked so well before. He strikes the rock. God immediately calls out Moses's presumption as a lack of trust, and it costs him the opportunity to lead the people into the Promised Land.

There is a poetry and artistry to God's movement that not only reflects his character but preserves the glory for himself. When he breathes life into a situation, he does so in varied ways, making it nearly impossible for us to take credit for working a system or discovering a secret. We're left to marvel at it and praise the architect of it.

Analysts and engineer types struggle with this. There's an incessant quest to discover repeatable patterns and reproducible models, to reduce life to formulas. Ministry runs so much easier if we can simply find the right equation and apply it. But life-change, and the church as God's spiritual instrument for enacting it, is far more art than science.

YOU CAN'T DISSECT WONDER

I happen to believe that baseball is the greatest game on earth. No other sport so perfectly combines athleticism and artistry, team and individual competition, intelligence and power.

But purists have grieved over recent tendencies in Major League Baseball, as sabermetrics and analytics have largely robbed the game of its human component. Every minute aspect of professional baseball is now analyzed, computerized, and subjected to algorithms and diagnostics. It's all about exit velocities and launch angles, spin rates and overshifts, UZR, wOBA, wRC+, and WAR; mathematical formula has all but replaced instinct and gut feeling.

And that's a shame. Because you might not be able to discredit the science of the BABIP, but you lose the beauty and virtuosity of the hit and run, the suicide squeeze, and the double switch.

I think God is an old-school baseball fan. There's a wonder and mystery to how he works, a creativity that defies explanation when he chooses to breathe life into one effort but allows another to lay lifeless, offering no explanation or reason.

What that means for church planting is that you can organize a church to death, but you can't organize one to life. All the steps and strategies and proven methods can be implemented to a T, but unless God decides to breathe on it, it will simply lay there like so much circuitry minus the power source. To borrow from the legend Jesus encountered in John 9, you can't stir up the healing waters of the Pool of Bethesda; you can only hang out nearby and jump in when the angel arrives to make a splash.

THE WONDER OF YOUR UNIQUE ADVENTURE

Ask any veteran church planter to relay the most memorable stories of his journey. What you'll hear will be the unscripted, unexpected, and unplanned—the turns in the road that popped up out of nowhere but became key factors in the movement forward.

Your best stories will equally come out of left field. A catalytic believer relocates to the area and joins your effort because she just happened to run into one of your core people at the grocery store. Another church updates all its AV equipment and calls out of the blue to see if you want any of their used stuff. A tragedy hits the middle school, and one of the parents mentions your availability to serve as a crisis counselor, which leads to a rash of opportunities. Your most unforgettable tales will range from astonishing to bizarre, but none will have been in your strategic plan.

In the aftermath of the 9/11 terrorist attacks, two things occurred in our city that significantly affected our church plant. First, our municipal officials turned to some of the local clergy to ask for help in a citywide rally at the local high school football stadium the following night, to offer a gathering place for coping and community support. Someone told the organizers I was a native of New York City and had witnessed the Twin Towers being built. The next thing I knew, I was invited to speak at the gathering. An event that, forty-eight hours earlier, no one could have fathomed happening afforded me an opportunity to present the gospel to a crowd of thousands at a time of desperate longing for hope. Multiple people came to Christ in the days following that gathering, and some became part of our fledgling church.

The second effect came about over time. Following the attacks, the resulting economic downturn precipitated a hardware store chain's decision to close their location in our town. They wanted a quick sale of their building, and two months later, we found ourselves under contract to buy a 35,000-square-foot building smack-dab on the main drag of the city for use as a permanent facility. A series of further wondrous events followed, including a half-million-dollar gift toward renovations donated by a guy who had actually left our church a few months earlier. Just like that, we secured a permanent place to use as an outpost of the gospel, facilitated through the horrific actions of Christ-opposing terrorists in another part of the nation. What they intended for evil, God used for good.

Weird, crazy stuff. I remember thinking, *You hear stories like this, but it's always someone else who experiences it, never me.* And then it was my turn.

You can't script that. It doesn't come as a result of working the plan. You can't predict it, manufacture it, or even prepare for it. It just happens, because an unpredictable God delights in introducing wild variations that make the ride maddening and wondrous at the same time.

One phrase became a sort of mantra through our church planting years: "The thrill of the adventure is more in its retelling than in its living." In the midst of the story, we see little resemblance to our plans and models. The pace and twists don't match the script; they feel random and out of control. But the God who defiantly refuses to follow a pattern or repeat the same story twice incorporates unique adventure moments into each individual story that we'll throw up our hands over in living but thrill in retelling.

WORK YOUR PLAN, JUST DON'T BANK ON IT

The point here is not to ignore quality resources or to embark without a strategy. You need to have a plan. To do so will lay down tracks to run on and provide an essential framework for priorities and focus. My colleague Jay Nickless has designed the best church planting training track I've ever seen; it establishes a clear path and anticipates multiple adjustments as God unfurls his own plan. I'd recommend it to anyone. Yes, by all means, select a method that matches your vision. Stick with it, and work it passionately.

Just don't expect the plan to play out the way it's scripted. Write your timelines and projections in pencil, not ink. Lead, invest, trust, and stay faithful. And then . . . watch for the unscripted surprises. They're guaranteed to come, and *they* will be what defines your journey and displays God's playful creativity.

Church planting in the real world will never go by the book . . . except the unique one you write after you're done.

CHAPTER 3

THE TRUTH ABOUT GETTING "BUTTS IN SEATS"

or

What You Do to Bring Them,
You'll Have to Do to Keep Them

Comedian Tim Allen once told of how his wife blew up their car's engine by letting the oil run out. He questioned how she could let it happen. "Didn't the oil light go on?" he asked. She replied matter-of-factly, "Uh . . . yes!" His response? "Not expecting the truth, I was stunned."[1]

A renowned church planting guru was asked at a gathering of planters to name the single most important requirement for successfully planting a church. He replied matter-of-factly, "Butts in seats." The audience gasped, not just in shocked surprise that he believed it, but that he would come right out and say it. Not expecting the truth, they were stunned.

Denominations and sending churches wax eloquent about how new churches should be established through intense prayer, bridge building with lost people, and living out the love of Christ in the midst of a dark world. But follow the money, the benchmark charts, and the report forms, and the smoky rhetoric clears to reveal what most regard as the actual key: get people in the door.

This occurs for understandable reasons. When pursuing the critical mass and financial base necessary to keep a church alive, plants experience consistent mathematical patterns. Attendance at the launch service will decline by 25 to 50 percent in week two and then follow a steady downward trajectory before bottoming out at approximately week six, at which time the inverted bell curve can be expected to turn upward before settling in at around 75 percent of the initial service's number. If that number stabilizes at or above critical mass, the church will survive. If not, its chances are slim.

The numbers don't lie. If you want viability at the end, you must drive sufficient turnout at the beginning. It's basic math.

ASSUMED PRIORITY ONE: CAPTURE AN AUDIENCE

A vacuum salesman knocked on our door and asked to give us a demonstration. I thought it was a joke. I'd always assumed door-to-door salesmen became extinct in the 1960s. Turns out it's still very much a thing.

We told him we weren't in the market and couldn't afford a new vacuum anyway, but he said he receives credit for the sheer number of demonstrations he completes, whether the person buys or not, so we agreed to help him out (and yes, we knew that itself was a sales technique . . . we weren't born yesterday).

After his thorough—and excruciatingly long—demonstration, we politely reiterated we wouldn't be making a purchase. But we'd developed enough rapport with him that as he packed up, he revealed a bit of insider information. If he can get to the demonstration, he said, regardless how definitively the homeowner had stated his or her lack of interest, one out of every three would buy the vacuum cleaner.

I was amazed . . . and impressed. That's a fantastic return rate. And on a huge ticket item. I still didn't purchase the machine, but I thought, *No wonder they keep doing it this way.* In fact, one of the most famous and long-standing American vacuum manufacturers, the Kirby Company, still sells its vacuums exclusively through in-home demonstrations.

Exposure—and repeated exposure—has been proven to be *the* pivotal element in influencing consumer behavior. People must be persuaded to try the establishment and then convinced by the merchandise, service, or experience to become a return customer. Repeated exposure increases the probability of loyal patronage. A predictable percentage of those who visit will return, and another predictable percentage of returnees will become regulars.

That formula extends to involvement in a new church.

Before you cough up a fur ball over how terribly unspiritual that sounds, keep in mind how Scripture underscores the importance of creating an audience with lost people so they'll have the chance to respond to the gospel. "How can they believe in him if they have never heard about him?" Paul wrote. "And how can they hear about him unless someone tells them?" (Romans 10:14–15 NLT). Jesus performed some impressive feats for the sole purpose of establishing credibility and drawing his countrymen's attention so he could deliver his message to them. The greater the exposure, the greater the opportunity for impact.

Which brings us back to the prevailing wisdom: it's all about the butts. Get them there, and keep them coming. The hope, of course, is that by returning regularly, the individual will have repeated exposure to the gospel, eventually recognize his or her need for Christ, and be prompted by the Spirit to respond in genuine faith.

AROUSE THE SENSES, OFFER A BENEFIT, SATISFY A CRAVING

To optimize traffic flow, the church planting world has adopted a paradigm of need satisfaction and buzz creation. Communicate that the church is here to meet needs, and that participation will be rewarded with excellence and benefits that make the return well worth the investment. Find what most grabs the target audience's attention and offer it. Benefit them. Intrigue them. Entice them.

So we sponsor Christmas Spectaculars, Mom's Day Outs, and free concerts in the park. We serve gourmet coffee in the lobby and promote cleverly titled message series. We offer exercise classes, book clubs, job fairs, and sports leagues. The more extravagant and appealing the offerings, the greater the anticipated return.

Knowing how the lives of suburban American parents revolve around their kids, during one Easter week, three different church plants in our community promoted egg hunts. But none simply handed out empty bags and flung eggs around the playground. One advertised a "world record" number of candy eggs to be scattered across a park lawn. A second announced Easter eggs would be launched by a giant explosion out of the "world's largest Easter egg." At a third, a local TV news crew would cover the event as Easter eggs were dropped from a hovering helicopter (I'm not making this up). At all three, the parents received slickly designed flyers inviting them to Easter services the following weekend while their kids pinballed off each other in the throes of a major sugar rush.

On another occasion, a church rented a large billboard near the freeway and promoted a big event featuring a local celebrity. The sign announced that every first-time visitor would be automatically registered in a drawing for an assortment of fabulous prizes, including iPads, laptops, and the grand prize—a trip to

Hawaii. They had done their research—giveaways are shown to be among the most effective tools to drive commercial traffic. And they were right; more than two thousand people showed up for the chance to win.

Just get the butts in the seats.

THE ENTITLEMENT EFFECT

Those examples may either turn your stomach or send you scrambling to try it yourself, but what they don't do is divulge the long-term effect the "butts in seats" approach produces.

When enticement is established as the foremost basis for church participation, maintaining the same level of stimulation becomes a condition for continued involvement. It's the next dirty little secret of contemporary church planting: What you do to bring them is what you'll have to do to keep them.

Enticement breeds expectation, which gives birth to entitlement. And entitlements, once bestowed, become nearly impossible to withdraw. Think of Social Security, Medicare, and DACA. What begins as a benefit inevitably morphs into an inalienable right.

Nicholas Eberstadt wrote in *A Nation of Takers* that half of all American households now receive some form of entitlement, and entitlement spending accounts for a full two-thirds of the federal budget. Americans, he says, have become more and more "addicted to and enslaved by entitlements."[2]

We reason that once our seat-fillers meet Christ, God will begin the process of transforming them from takers into givers. But we've unwittingly fostered an addiction. As soon as we attempt to wean them from it, they move on to another supplier, concluding that this church "just doesn't meet my needs anymore."

We've seduced them with consumerism and, in the process, commercialized the gospel. The church, intended to be the holy carrier of God's very Spirit, is reduced to a commodity existing to satisfy temporal cravings for the small price of return business.

Enticement becomes the pimp that prostitutes the bride of Christ.

NO SUBSTITUTES

Thomas Edison said, "There is no substitute for hard work."

Bear Bryant said, "There's no substitute for guts."

Steven Spielberg said, "There is no substitute for going out to the movies."

Some things can simply never be substituted. In the real world of church planting, the same unexciting, time-consuming practices are still the only substantive means to seeing lost people reached.

I meant it when I said this wouldn't be a how-to book on church planting, so this is as close as I'll get to breaking that promise. At the core of genuinely reaching unchurched people, you'll find the same three basic disciplines: pray-pray-pray, train-train-train, and engage-engage-engage.

Pray-Pray-Pray

This is where your eyes naturally skip to the next section, because it's a given. You don't want to waste your time hearing about your need to pray. You get it.

Stop for a moment before you do that and admit with me that you kind of see prayer as a necessary but perfunctory part of your action plan. *Of course* we need to pray, and we do. But we'd rather check it off the list and get on to the stuff that actually makes a difference.

It took me a long time to admit I considered consistent, focused prayer an indirect rather than direct contributor to gaining an audience with real, living, spiritually disinterested people. Sure,

I could pray for opportunities to cross paths with those ready to hear the gospel, but what I really needed to do was get out there and pound the pavement.

I honestly believe one of the key differences between our failed church plant and our fruitful one was someone who showed me otherwise.

Ardith Rupp didn't even live in our town, but I met her when I spoke at her church about our planting project. She came up afterward and said she was committing to pray every single day for God to open doors for us to meet and reach lost people.

Ardith didn't just offer a token commitment; she actually prayed. Every day. She'd occasionally contact me to tell me what she was praying. And stuff started happening. I didn't even connect it at first, but I'd have a crazy encounter with a random person leading to a spiritual conversation, and I'd learn Ardith had been praying for that to happen that day. It became more than coincidence. It almost seemed like a game. I'd have an important meeting, and I'd find out Ardith felt prompted to pray for me at that moment without even knowing what I was doing.

We reshaped our approach to our prayer team because of Ardith. Yes, we should have done it the first go-round, but this time it whacked me upside the head hard enough to make me treat it as more than obligatory. I started communicating with our prayer supporters more regularly and even started praying more specifically myself.

Call it coincidence if you like, but when I and others in our core consciously and specifically prayed for lost people we knew, or for opportunities to meet ones we didn't yet know, things just . . . happened. Strange things. We'd have chance encounters with people who revealed a need we could meet. We'd see sudden turns in conversations from safe topics like weather and sports to unprovoked revelations of longing or pain, with an openness to answers. We'd get out-of-the-blue questions about why we believe what we believe or how the church was doing.

Let me simplify this for you with one type of prayer to build into your lifestyle and into the parlance of your core group interactions. In Colossians 4:2–4, Paul uses a word translated "watchful" for the evangelistic prayer he invites his readers to. That word doesn't just mean non-dozy. It means an accompanying alertness—prayer attached to a conscious, raised antenna for noticing how God will move to enact it afterward.

He then couples that with the picture of a door opening—a theme repeated often in his travels and writings. He reported to the Antioch believers how God had opened a door for them to share the gospel with the Gentiles (Acts 14:27). In 1 Corinthians 16:8–9, he spoke of how God opened a door in Ephesus. In 2 Corinthians 2:12, he said the Lord had opened a door in Troas.

Paul might have been using a double meaning in his letter to the Colossians, because he was imprisoned at the time and would certainly be enhanced by being freed from the prison doors. But it's clear he believed that God can be asked to open doors of opportunity. Commenting on this passage, John Piper wrote, "I take him to mean when Christians pray, God changes circumstances and attitudes and receptivity for the Word so that instead of hitting a brick wall, the Word finds an open door and becomes unusually effective."[3]

Practically, this means keeping prayer for lost people at the forefront of groups and community gatherings. Let it be specific, anticipatory prayer—the kind that departs from the prayer time actively looking for doors to swing open in the hours and days to follow.

Be honest, do you tend to tack prayer for lost people on to the end of small group meetings, sometimes never getting to it? Is it a list that gets introduced and then more or less winds up buried in a drawer somewhere? Elevate prayer, specifically prayer for divinely opened doors and for the souls of individual, named people you want to see God reach.

Yes, I know this is nothing you don't already know. But for me, there's a difference between what I intellectually comprehend and what I truly believe and actually do. Which is it for you?

Train-Train-Train

Fair warning: lifestyle evangelism training is the least popular equipping you'll do. There's no easy way to say this—most people just don't want to be stretched to share their faith. And they're especially reluctant to turn out for training on how to do so. They know they're inevitably going to be challenged, or even held accountable, to actually do something they consider uncomfortable.

We know equipping the saints for the work of the ministry is central to our role as pastors. We just get frustrated when no one wants to learn to reach the lost. Announce a parenting clinic or a spin class, and you may have to start a waiting list. But offer a personal evangelism course or a workshop on how to start a seeker Bible study, and . . . crickets. People would rather have their eyebrows waxed.

The most natural thing in the world to do in response to that is to cut your losses and stop beating your head against the wall. But don't. Remember that the level to which God's people will respond doesn't determine the priority of what we call them to.

Jesus lamented how the pipers played the pipe for people, but no one would dance (Matthew 11:17). Get used to that, by the way. That's what will often happen when you repeatedly trumpet the need for everybody to be on point to deliver the gospel message to those in their world. But keep banging that drum. Keep training. Keep talking about your personal experiences doing it. Keep reminding people that they're more than welcome to invite guests to come to church services and events with them, but the primary way people around them will hear the story of the cross is through one of their trusted friends who has experienced its transforming effect.

As you do, keep a couple of things in mind. First, there isn't a silver bullet of personal evangelism training methods—one that sustains motivation and excitement. It doesn't exist. Every program has a half-life of effectiveness, so you can fully expect less response and enthusiasm as you repeat the same training opportunities. Vary them, redesign them, repackage them, and know it will always be an upstream swim to get people to participate.

But don't stop.

And second, with all the emphasis these days on missional community, be careful that serving in the name of Jesus doesn't become a substitute for articulating the cross of Jesus. One of the missional community strategy's trends has been that a lot of good service happens, but it doesn't always translate into transformed lives or repentance from sin. Missional community activity needs to be attached to message delivery. If it doesn't, it devolves into social gospel.

Regardless of the mode of training you use—weekend seminars, small groups, Sunday school classes, missional communities, retreats, conferences—don't let twelve months pass without overtly offering lifestyle evangelism training again. Keep it front and center. Continue to invite your people to it. The return will never seem to match the investment, but if we want to see lost people receive the gift, it's the found people who will deliver it.

Engage-Engage-Engage

There's a simple, undeniable fact about evangelizing those far from God. To reach them, you've got to be in proximity to them. That doesn't happen through token events where you visit skid row and then congratulate yourself on your courageous outreach ministry. It happens when people live regular, daily lives integrating with those whose values and lifestyles are significantly different than their own. It happens when they overtly choose to live and work and play with people outside their faith family.

In terms of outreach, this doesn't mean knocking on strangers' doors or handing out tracts to passersby on the street. It means being in sustained, close, relational connection with those whose values and lifestyles are more than likely significantly different than yours. Finding common ground, genuinely caring, uniting around shared causes. Engaging.

We know the natural tendency: Christians are inclined to cloister. And when they do, outreach becomes relegated to advertising. Let the flyer or the social media post or the community announcement serve as the invitation to "those lost people out there" to come to an event where they can hear how they can be saved.

The only way to fight that is to intentionally lead our core believers to consciously avoid isolating themselves. Don't let the church softball team join a church league; have them play in the local beer league. Resist the urge to put up a community board limited to advertising Christian hairdressers, realtors, or mechanics. Encourage believers to engage with regular people they encounter every day. Tom Mercer has written how everyone has a circle of eight to fifteen people who are already in their world, for whom they are on the front lines to represent Christ.[4] We don't need our people to "reach the whole world"; we just need them to engage those whose world they already share.

You need to lead this by example. It can't happen from safe vantage points like behind your pulpit or a keyboard. Most church planters spend progressively less time with unbelievers the longer they lead their church. Your list of ten closest friends should always include multiple unbelievers. Does it?

OF EGG HUNTS AND SEAT FILLERS

I later had the chance to talk with all three of the planters whose churches had done the big Easter egg events. In the days following the event, they were energized and inspired. Six months later, not a single visitor to any of their events had to their knowledge become part of their churches.

If you want lots of buzz and the perception of momentum, do whatever it takes to get butts in seats. Tap into felt needs; offer benefits and exhilaration in exchange for attendance. Then deal with the perpetual pressure to keep entertaining and enticing them enough to retain those butts, in the hope that some will eventually be transformed into Christ followers.

But if you want to be free from enslavement to entitlement, if you want substantive impact and Christ transformation, get used to the fact that the same old, long-sustained practices of consistent prayer for open doors, equipping believers as gospel proclaimers, and relationship building with lost people are what outreach has always been about, and always will be.

There is no substitute.

CHAPTER 4

THE TRUTH ABOUT CORE GROUPS AND LAUNCH TEAMS

or

No One's Ever as Committed as You

Brandon (not his real name) was a key cog in our first daughter church plant's leadership core.

He'd lost his wife to cancer while still a young man and was raising their little girl on his own. But he had also dedicated himself to serving Jesus and was all-in to make a difference in his world. A very likeable and multitalented guy, he had a knack for building solid relationships, enjoyed tremendous success as a sales rep, and played a wicked bass guitar.

Brandon remarried—a terrific, Christ-loving woman—and I had the privilege of performing their wedding. I was stoked when Brandon sensed God's prompting to become part of the nucleus that stepped up to plant our daughter church. He made fast friends with our church planter and was incredibly responsive to the continuing leadership development being poured into him. We envisioned him becoming one of the new church's first elders.

Two weeks before the plant's official launch date, our church planter called with bombshell news. Brandon's new wife had discovered a trail of receipts that revealed a completely hidden lifestyle. For years spanning both of his marriages, he had regularly hired prostitutes during his business travels. He'd engaged in an array of deviant sexual activity that would make Hefner blush. He'd masked thousands of dollars spent on wanton immoral behavior. His life was largely a lie.

The revelation detonated like a roadside bomb. Brandon was deeply embedded in the church planting effort, and the news decimated the entire project. Besides having to navigate the devastating effects on his wife and daughter—while somehow maintaining a modicum of love and compassion for Brandon himself (no small feat given how overtly he had deceived us all)—we were left performing triage on the church planting endeavor. In an instant, the entire focus, strategy, and timeline lurched off its axis. We regrouped as best we could, but the explosion hit so close to the control center and the impact was so sudden and intense that the plant never fully recovered.

This sounds like a one-off, a Bizarro World scenario where Satan discovers and exploits a hidden weakness to sabotage what would otherwise have been a solid plan. But while the example is extreme, the underlying reality is universal. Core groups and launch teams are essential to a church plant, but they're also far more volatile and unstable than we ever anticipate.

Every church planting strategy I've ever seen (including the efforts I coach) includes the vital early step of assembling a core of faithful believers—a launch team that will form the effort's backbone. The blueprint is reasonable and logical:

- Prayerfully seek those who will respond to the call to stretch their faith and join the mission.

- Personally recruit pioneers and risk-takers, including some who may even consider relocating to the target area.
- Issue invitations in multiple venues for those who possess essential gifts and can fill crucial roles.
- Look for unaffiliated believers already living in the target area to complete the team.
- Challenge, envision, organize, and equip the team members to sacrifice their time, energy, and money and to hone their skills to penetrate the community and catalyze spiritual movement.

If a sending church fully commits to taking new territory and setting up a church plant effort for success, it will not only encourage a significant number of its people to join this core, but it will release its brightest and best to seed it. J. D. Greear's *Gaining by Losing* rings that bell loudly:

> Churches that take Jesus' promises and the Great Commission seriously are committed to sending out some of their best leaders into the mission . . .
>
> God calls his leaders, not to a platform to build a great ministry *for* themselves, but to an altar where they die *unto* themselves. This means sending out our best with abandon.[1]

Church planting is a team sport, and you want your best players taking the field.

WHAT YOU EXPECT VERSUS WHAT YOU GET

On paper, the concept of a vibrant and motivated core group looks fantastic. The church planter serves as a leader of leaders; the team unifies under the banner of a singular purpose; and stories of faith-rewarding impact fuel ongoing advances. If we could script everyone's life for them and direct their every move and decision, it would work like a charm. It's a surefire strategy . . . on paper.

But in the real world, scissors cuts paper. What you expect from a launch team is enthusiasm, commitment, sacrifice, and unity; what you get is something entirely different.

Balls begin to drop. People don't follow through. Others bow out. A family determines they want to return to the mother church. Tension arises between two individuals who decide it would be best if they weren't part of the same team anymore. Someone's job moves them away. Someone else simply stops showing up at all, without explanation.

Then the first of the big bombs goes off. A marriage is revealed to be teetering on the brink of divorce. A hidden addiction comes to light. A key leader abruptly announces he's done with church altogether.

Because church planters are usually optimists, they tend to believe that people who commit to the core group will hold true to their pledge. And because planters are also egotists, they generally believe that their superlative leadership skills will galvanize these same people into a cohesive, finely tuned fighting force.

FIVE UNIVERSAL TRUTHS

Those beliefs inevitably collide head-on with a set of five universal truths about core groups and launch teams, all of which are guaranteed to demand your energy and slow your pace:

1. **There's unrevealed sin.** Every closet has its skeletons, and spiritual movement tends to open the doors to expose them. God sees to it. When there's sin in the camp, he finds ways to reveal it so that cleansing and repentance can take place. Moses warned

the advancing nation of Israel that "your sin will find you out" (Numbers 32:23). It's not a question of *if* significant dark history and habits will come out; it's a matter of *when*. Even the godliest of your launch team members are harboring secrets and addictions that God will allow to be brought to light.

2. **There are hidden agendas.** Getting in on the ground floor represents opportunity. Some of the first volunteers to a church plant project bring a long-term, deep conviction about how something in the church should be done, or what they personally should get to do. They've just never been given the platform to do it. The new church provides that platform, at least in their minds.

Hidden agendas are seldom discovered early in the process. They show up later, after the person has entrenched himself in what he believes is the inner circle. For some, it may be a desire for a paid position on the new church's staff. For some, it may be the development of a pet ministry or a point role leading (and controlling) an existing one. For others, it may be a seat at the decision-makers' table or the expectation he will enjoy free access to you as the leader in ways he never could in the established church. Not everyone on a launch team carries such an agenda, but almost every launch team has at least one member who does.

3. **There are unstated conditions for continuing involvement.** Church planters can become victims of their own reputations and vision-casting skills. People love a winner, and some who jump into the adventure do so with an assumption your star will rise quickly and blaze brightly, with their wagon hitched to it. When it doesn't—when the unspoken expectation for how quickly the church will grow or how deeply it will satisfy their needs is not met—these people will be tested.

Many will fail that test. They'll give other reasons for dropping out. They'll point to the burdens of work or continuing education, the need for a more developed children's or youth program during their kids' critical formative years, or the uncontestable trump card—"We feel like God is leading us elsewhere." But at the root will sit a never-articulated condition you failed to meet.

The Rock and Roll Hall of Fame may never induct Rick Springfield for giving us "Jesse's Girl," but a line from another of his songs for some reason always plays in my mind when I encounter the unspoken expectations of launch team members: "You said someday I'd have a whole lotta money . . . but when that didn't happen overnight, I found out how much you really cared."[2]

As the leader, you are always on probation, even with your launch team members. Most fully believe they're sincere when they promise they're all-in. They have no idea they're carrying unconscious conditions . . . until they go unfulfilled.

4. There are very different meanings for the exact same words. When you paint a verbal picture of your new church's vision, you have a clear mental image of what you mean. But no matter how articulate and detailed you are in those descriptions, core group members can make fundamentally different associations using the exact same words.

You say your new church will play "contemporary worship music," and someone sees a folk guitarist on stage. You say you'll build "authentic community," and someone's mind pictures Sunday school potlucks. You say yours will be a church that "values children and families," and someone visualizes "Awana program." You say, "We want to do everything with quality," and someone hears, "We'll hire professional musicians for our worship team."

When our church decided to move toward purchasing a permanent facility, we repeated the same maxim until we were blue in the face: we will never be a building-centric church. We'd use it as a corporate worship center, but we were committed to keeping outreach and ministry in the real world. We declared that Bible studies and small groups would continue meeting in neighborhoods. We wanted outreach to happen in coffee shops, offices, homes, and community centers. We would allow the building to sit empty most of the week to retain our vision and identity.

Everybody cheered.

Six months after moving into our facility, one of our core team members announced he was leaving because we weren't utilizing the building to start new programs. We weren't acting as "good stewards," he said. He was shocked—*shocked*—to see us wasting the resource God had given us.

As the verbal descriptions you use with your core team begin to take physical form, the radical difference between how you define the words you use and how your core people understand them exposes itself. Some will complain loudly; some will develop a low-grade fever of disappointment; others will simply drift away feeling misled.

5. There's a reason dechurched Christians stay that way. Each time we planted, we prayerfully sought out believers who were already living in our target area. Because we were committed not to steal sheep, we limited those searches to Christians who weren't currently connected to a local church. In theory, we believed there would be those who simply hadn't found the right place yet, and they would be responsive to the vision we were bringing for a vibrant church in their area.

We were sorely mistaken.

Meeting disconnected believers can start with such promise. We heard phrases like:

- "We've always wanted this kind of a church, but there's just nothing like it around here."

- "This is an answer to prayer! We've been longing for a church like this in our area."
- "This town desperately needs this kind of church."

But dechurched Christians can be fool's gold. Believers who deeply value the local church as God's instrument to advance his kingdom usually find a way to stay connected in one, even when they don't love everything about it. Those who skip from church to church, who claim to have been repeatedly victimized by them, who consistently drift uncommitted to any one group for long, often belie a heart-level problem sure to negatively influence your team.

Disgruntled church members are often simply disgruntled people. Many are perpetual faultfinders, "professional weaker brothers," control freaks. They make broad accusations like, "That group claimed to be Christlike, but they were judgmental hypocrites." A little digging often reveals "that group" attempted to address an issue in their life, and they didn't want to deal with it. So they've repeated the same pattern: focus on the negative, complain, withdraw, drift, and repeat. They creep back into the bushes until the next scapegoat ministry comes along.

There are profound exceptions to this, of course. You may happen upon a mature believer who recently relocated to the area or one who left a church after a healthy process because of a legitimate doctrinal shift or philosophical difference. But all too often, when you beat the bushes, nasty things fall out.

Please understand, the grace of Christ extends richly toward every one of these folks. He passionately loves them, values them, and yearns for their wholeness. There's a place in every church for those carrying baggage, and God's power can transform them in astounding ways. They just aren't going to be capable of forming the backbone of a core group in your early days.

HOPE FOR THE BEST,
PREPARE FOR THE WORST

Church planting manuals and organizations don't typically focus on the negative. Nobody likes a killjoy. But by remaining silent about almost universal launch team experiences, they leave unsuspecting church planters without a framework for responding when they emerge.

I wish someone would have given me a heads-up about them. But it needs to be said. You can pretty much count on every one of these things happening within your own core:

- Those quickest to commit will be among the earliest to drop out.
- Someone you least expect will defect in the first year.
- Someone on your core team will betray their marriage, church teachings, or your personal trust.
- People who come in criticizing their former church will one day go somewhere else and do the same about yours.
- None of your initial core people will still be with you five years later.

That last one stings, by the way. You'll insist your situation will be different. You *know* the people who have committed to your launch team. You've got history with them. You've invested deeply in them and have witnessed their loyalty. You've pinky sworn to raise your kids side by side, to lock arms for Jesus, to grow old serving him together.

And none of them will be there in five years. Yes, there are the occasional exceptions that prove the rule. But find a planting pastor still at the helm of his church after five years, and ask him to pull out a picture of the team at the first core meeting (if he had the foresight to take one). You'll discover there are "unique" stories behind where they all went. And they didn't all leave at once. Someone was transferred. Another went through a divorce. An unresolvable personal issue arose with this one (it was their fault). That one felt they needed something the plant couldn't offer. The stories vary, but the bottom line remains the same: five years later, they'll all be gone.

My purpose in telling you this is not to jade you toward your launch team or discourage your investment in them; it's to mitigate your being blindsided when it happens to you. And to offer you some hope as you walk through it.

IT HAPPENED TO THE BEST

Take solace in the fact that when it comes to core group disappointment, you're in good company. If Jesus had set out to market his school of core group training, he probably wouldn't have won a lot of applicants. Let's face it, his track record was less than stellar. Twelve recruits, a three-year residency—and these were the marks of his core team members:

- They consistently didn't grasp his basic principles.
- They routinely challenged his methods.
- They slept through the most important class.
- Two had their mother, of all people, waltz into the classroom and argue for better grades.
- One pulled a knife on those who opposed him.
- The entire team repeatedly failed tests of loyalty and character.
- Every last one of them bailed out when the project was threatened.
- One sold him out completely and then committed suicide.

None of that would look very good on the brochure.

The apostle Paul's success rate wasn't any better. His very first recruit (John Mark) quit the team midseason (Acts 13:13; 15:38). An argument with his primary partner (Barnabas) led to a falling out that was never resolved (Acts 15:37–40). Sickness sidelined one of his team members (2 Timothy 4:20); another abandoned him (4:10); and when the going got tough, in his own words, Paul reported, "Everyone deserted me" (4:16).

The best in the business, including the very Son of God, struggled with their core teams. When it happens to you, it's not an indicator you did something poorly or chose the wrong people; it's simply a reality of human nature in a fallen world.

WHAT TO DO ABOUT IT

What are you supposed to do with all this? You can't plant a church without core members. You need a foundation of committed Christians to energize and implement the plan to reach the lost. You certainly don't want to be skewed in your view of people or expect the worst from them. Pessimism kills risk-taking and entrepreneurship.

A few adjustments can go a long way toward keeping us away from the ledge when the inevitable happens and our launch team proves to be wobbly.

1. **Expect regular attrition.** In God's "army," every enlisted soldier has a designated tour of duty. Some will prove to be shorter, some longer. God knows in advance how long each recruit's tour will last, but *he never tells* in advance which will be which. Each member of your launch team will serve an important purpose in the overall life of the church, but few, if any, will serve a tour of duty as long as yours. Celebrate them when they're with you, anticipate regular transition, and grant them an honorable discharge when they move on.

2. Invest consistently in a pipeline of future leaders. When you expect turnover and attrition, you're wise to always be developing understudies and leaders-in-training. One of the biggest leadership mistakes church planters make is recruiting team leaders with the mind-set that if they simply place the right person in the right slot, he or she will take it from there and relieve the planter of the need to manage further.

Training and leadership development must never stop, even among those who are fully trained and excelling. Championship teams are never built without giving attention to the depth chart, preparing for the inevitable "next man up" moments when the team suffers loss or injury. As the leader, you must always be looking for the next generation, the next trainee to step up when the current generation falls or needs a break.

You need to know that this will slow your progress considerably. You'll wish you could crank up productivity and harvest to the next level and not be saddled with reaching back just to retrain and redevelop those you've already trained once. Deal with it; it's part and parcel of leadership in a healthy organization. God's Spirit has always been willing to slow down for you. You need to do the same for others.

3. Get used to disappointment. In our family, nary a day goes by without us quoting multiple lines from the classic movie *The Princess Bride* (in our defense, Google "most quotable movies of all time" and see what happens). One of the more memorable comes when Inigo Montoya asks the masked man to reveal his identity. The man declines to do so. "I simply must know," Inigo insists. The masked man replies, "Get used to disappointment."[3]

The simple fact is, you will be routinely disappointed by your core team. No matter how effectively you cast vision and train them, no matter how enthusiastically they voice their loyalty and allegiance, no one will ever be as committed to your church plant as you are. No one else will work half as hard, sacrifice half as much, or care half as deeply as you.

You can bemoan that fact and allow resentment to fester toward those who fail to share your commitment—which will be everyone. Or you can get used to disappointment and cut them loose from any unrealistic expectation.

In a quote widely attributed to Martin Luther King Jr., he said, "We must accept finite disappointment, but never lose infinite hope." People will regularly disappoint you, but God never gives up hope for them. The one who began a good work in them has promised he will be faithful to complete it until the day of Christ Jesus (Philippians 1:6). What does that mean, if not that he keeps his own vision for us alive even while seeing reason to be disappointed?

4. Accept the commitments people are willing to give, without begrudging the ones they aren't. Scholars have long debated the significance of the words for *love* used by John when reporting Jesus and Peter's shoreline exchange in John 21. Three times, Jesus asks Peter if he loves him, and three times, Peter replies in the affirmative.

The Greek text records Jesus' use of the term *agape*—generally understood as the highest level of love—in his first two inquiries. Peter replies that he does love Jesus, but he uses the word *phileo*—a brotherly love conveying affection but not the ultimate, covenantal level of *agape*. When Jesus poses his question the third time, the text records him ceding to the word Peter had used: "Do you *phileo* me?"

Jesus and Peter most likely spoke Aramaic rather than Greek in their original exchange, so whether or not the use of different Greek words for *love* carries major significance—I personally believe it does—no one can be quite sure. But one thing in the passage *is* sure. Jesus never shames Peter for his past denials and never expresses a hint of disappointment at the level of commit-ment Peter is able to offer. After each response, Jesus gives Peter an equal assignment, fully commissioning him to a position of trust.

It's true that God refers to his people as sheep, known to be among the weakest, most vulnerable, and least intelligent of ani-mals (more on that in the next chapter). But he cherishes them. He loves and rejoices over them. He doesn't demand they become lions or elephants. He receives what they can offer as sheep and guides them with a full heart.

Jesus asked Peter to feed his sheep, but he also knew Peter was still one himself. And he was apparently okay with that.

Your core people may have made promises they can't keep, but you aren't called to judge them on that scale. View them with grace. Grant them the same love and respect the lover of their souls pours over them. Challenge them to new heights and invite them to high commitment, but release them from demands and gladly accept whatever they are able to give. Your angst and frustration will melt, and your core group will see a much clearer picture of their Father's heart toward them.

CHAPTER 5

THE TRUTH ABOUT
THE BACK DOOR

or

Don't Chase Christians

H enry Blackaby spoke to a gathering of pastors I attended in the heyday of his bestselling book *Experiencing God*. Reflecting on his own pastoral history in Saskatoon, Canada, in his sincere, grandfatherly way, he urged young pastors to stay faithful, to love their flocks, and to invest their whole hearts into the people under their care.

Then he said something that gave me one of those, "Wait, I couldn't have heard that right" moments. He said in all his years of pastoring that way, he didn't lose a single one of the sheep entrusted to him.

Immediately after the session ended, a church planter asked if we could talk and confided in me how demoralized he was by those words. They had hit him with a tidal wave of inadequacy and shame . . . because he *had* lost sheep. A ton of them. He'd seen a steady stream of people flow out the proverbial back door of his church. If he had been doing it right, he reasoned, that wouldn't have happened. He walked away feeling like an utter failure.

I could relate.

I certainly respect Henry Blackaby, and if he indeed served his entire pastoral career without seeing a single church member drop out, I give him props. But I've got to tell you, that has *not* at all been my experience. The back door has always stood wide open and often used, no matter how much effort I put into shutting it.

Church in general, and church plants in particular, have consistently faced the maddening challenge of retaining the people who find their way in. We often said we'd actually planted a megachurch, if you counted everybody who came in the front door and went out the back.

Plenty of attempts have been made to learn why that happens so commonly. William Hendricks's major study, compiled in his book *Exit Interviews*, reported reasons ranging from relational conflicts to institutional distrust.[1] But regardless of the reasons it happens, we church planters can't help but take it personally when it does. There are so few hooks on which to hang blame, and every hook is directly attached to us.

The dropouts may say, "Oh, we were just visiting," or "We were looking for something a little closer to home," but the fact remains they probably wouldn't have put the effort into coming in the first place if there wasn't a chance they'd see enough to keep them coming back. When they don't, it means we didn't deliver something they were looking for. And that finger points directly toward us, since everything from the preaching, to the children's areas, to the way they were welcomed, falls under our direction and responsibility.

Early in our Ohio church plant, we heard through the grapevine that a woman who had been very involved had decided to "move on." We'd built a close connection with her. She joined our small group, and I walked her fiancé and her through intensive counseling and then officiated their wedding. When the house they were moving into needed major renovation, we spent multiple days busting our guts in 90-degree heat tearing out her kitchen floor. We attended her daughter's sporting events and spent countless hours building community with her. The news she was leaving sucker punched me.

Because we had such direct bonds, my wife and I contacted her to see if what we had heard was true. She confirmed it was. Confused, we let her know how affected we were to hear it and asked what prompted her decision. She shrugged it off and said, "It's no big deal. People change churches all the time. Don't take it personally."

Don't take it personally? How else was I supposed to take it?

Oh, I know all the appropriate responses to that question: the church is God's, not ours; God has a plan for everyone's life, and we need to be kingdom-minded when he moves them to another assignment. I know I'm supposed to be noble and humble and open-handed and trusting. But I also got really ticked off.

There's a dark road I can go down whenever another person casually pulls out after all the investment, sacrifice, care, and giving that has been channeled in their direction. I'm torn between doing everything in my power to change his or her mind and hardening my heart in resentment to cope with the sense of betrayal and abandonment.

I'm not sure which is worse—the long-time attendee who decides he's had all the fun he can stand, the person who comes consistently for a month or two then concludes it's not for him, or the visitor who shows up once or twice and is never heard from again.

No one likes back door exits, but the effect is amplified in church plants for a couple reasons. First, there's the holy reason. We've prayed, invested, built trust, and finally see someone come to check out what we do. They hear the message of the gospel and experience the presence and community of God. We desperately want them to respond, to see their life changed and their destiny forever altered. When they finally witness what our entire mission has been designed to help them see and then just sniff at it and move on to the next thing, it leaves us with a soul-piercing pain.

And then there's the not-so-holy reason. Defections especially wound church planters because a church plant desperately *needs* people to stick around. Especially in the early, pioneering days, committed contributors are like gold. We need more of them, not less. If one or two families leave, the church's very survival can be threatened. Dropouts feel like death blows.

The back door pummels church planters. And the more it's used, the greater the intensity builds to do one thing: find a way to barricade it.

"SHUT DE DO, KEEP OUT DE DEBIL"

No small number of antidotes have been developed to cure the back-door disease. When I Googled "closing the back door of the church," these three entries stood atop the list of results:

- Five Incredible Steps to Close the Back Door in Your Church
- Four Keys to Closing the Back Door in Your Church
- 7 Ways to Close the Back Door of Your Church

The problem solvers tell us people fall through the cracks if they're not captured by involvement or relationship within a short amount of time. We therefore need to bridge the gaps between attending, connecting, and committing. We need to spread multiple nets to catch people before they fall away.

The suggested nets take a handful of common forms:

- assimilation pastor/personal contacts
- affinity groups and entry-level events
- small groups
- ministry teams
- connection points with the lead pastor/staff
- membership/orientation classes

Yet even when multiples of these systems are enacted, the common complaint among church planters remains: lots of people come, and lots of people go. We're left perpetually searching for the one elusive net that will catch and hold. The longer we're unable to find it, the more we're nagged by a sense of failure.

The False Presumption

Behind all this effort lies a largely unchallenged presumption: the cracks people fall through can and should be sealed, and we're both capable and responsible to seal them. As one church consultant put it, "It is critically important to guard the back door of the church." We're assured if we dedicate enough time, resources, and effort, we can stop people before they exit, and our improved retention rate will translate into increased attendance, giving, involvement, and—especially—life transformation.

But what if the solution we're searching for doesn't exist? What if we're pouring our resources into an unfillable sinkhole? I want to suggest the mandate to close the so-called back door is one Jesus never gave, and trying to do so is not only pointless but counterproductive.

Barring the Door Comes at a Price

There's a cost to attempting to stop attrition from a church plant. And there's a significant reason why it'll never work anyway.

First, consider the cost.

Since 1962, FDA regulations have required advertisers to disclose possible side effects when marketing drugs, which is why their TV ads always contain a litany of horrible things you could experience if you dare use them. If the same law applied to prescriptions for closing the church's back door, here are some side effects we might be required to list:

1. You'll grow unnecessarily exasperated. Every church will have those who clamor for something they insist is absolutely vital to keeping people around. A course. A program. An event. When they say, "What we need is . . ." they essentially mean, "What *you* need to provide is . . ." In order to placate them so they don't defect, you add their pet idea or program to your job description. You knuckle under, produce it, schedule it. And invariably those who clamored loudest don't bother showing up for it. But now you've got one more plate to spin, one more program to run.

It will drive you crazy.

2. You'll become enslaved to it. Once you establish the precedent of accepting the responsibility to provide whatever it takes to keep people coming back, you install that as your master. Every newcomer will bring in an additional set of expectations you'll be responsible to fulfill to prevent them from leaving, and you'll never be allowed to not provide it. Attendee retention is a fickle mistress. You won't be able to rest once you resign yourself to making it your duty. It will hold you hostage.

3. You'll reinforce a consumer mentality. Few phrases make my blood boil more than ones like this: "I stopped coming, and nobody even called." It's the epitome of entitled victimization. It implies you're expected to personally monitor every individual in your flock—to not only respond when they ask for help, but to notice if they test you with unannounced absences to see if you'll jump to prove your attentiveness and mollify their sensitivities.

As mentioned in chapter 3, consumerism flies directly in the face of Christ's character. But this one deserves to be teased out a bit more. Our culture is now fully ensconced in a customer-service-driven, Yelp-focused, "Would you say you received five-star service today?" ethos. It's all about the positive reviews, the social media Likes, the no-questions-asked return policies. When you cater to that, you reward the very self-absorption God wants to purge from our souls.

The apostle Paul made it exceptionally clear that while love will guide believers to mutually carry each other's burdens, it's each believer's responsibility to carry his own load (Galatians 6:2–5). The writer of Hebrews challenged Christ followers to "strengthen your feeble arms and weak knees" (Hebrews 12:12), to shift from self-service to others-orientation. He scolded believers who "ought to be teachers," but who were still acting as dependents (Hebrews 5:12).

If you spoon-feed people by accepting responsibility to ensure they're contented and won't threaten to leave, you'll create an environment where the baby birds simply sit in the nest with their beaks open, waiting for Mama to scout, retrieve, digest, and regurgitate the food, and then drop it into their mouths.

4. Anything you spend closing the back door can't be spent on your primary calling. One of the core principles of economics is called "opportunity cost"—which refers to "a benefit, profit, or value of something that must be given up to acquire or achieve something else."[2]

Put in real-world terms, if you spend $10 on a shirt, you can't spend it on lunch.

The same economics apply in church planting. You're called to invest your heart, time, and energy to see the lost found and the found matured. Every moment you spend designing and implementing mechanisms to retain people or prevent defection is one you can't spend on those prime directives.

The prophet Isaiah implied the same principle when he asked, "Why spend your money on food that does not give you strength? Why pay for food that does you no good?" (Isaiah 55:2 NLT). Jesus told Martha that Mary had chosen the "one thing worth being concerned about" when she resisted spending her energies on secondary priorities and instead sat at the feet of her Savior (Luke 10:42 NLT). When you expend your time and resources erecting barriers to prevent people from leaving, you burn fuel earmarked to drive your mission forward.

It Doesn't Work Anyway

Then we come to the reason we'll never be able to close the back door, irrespective of how hard we try. What I say next, I want to say very carefully—from a heart of love and respect—but also very honestly: Christians are sheep, and sheep never stop being sheep.

We're familiar with the spectrum of metaphors the Bible uses for God's people. They're a "body," a "tribe," an "army," "children," a "bride," and a "nation." But Jesus' favorite recurring term for them is "sheep." He refers to himself as a shepherd who cares for his sheep (John 10:11); he calls on Peter to feed his sheep (John 21:15–17); he says his sheep recognize his voice and know him (John 10:27). The New Testament uses imagery of tending sheep in the field to describe church leaders (Acts 20:28–29; 1 Peter 5:1–4).

This sounds very poetic and congenial. It makes for lovely Hallmark cards during Clergy Appreciation Month . . . until we realize what makes a sheep a sheep. Sheep can be cute and cuddly, but they're also dirty, smelly, dumb animals. They're well-documented as being among the neediest and most defenseless and unintelligent species of the animal kingdom.

David Murray, professor of Old Testament and theology at Puritan Reformed Theological Seminary, listed twelve characteristics of sheep:

1. Sheep are foolish.
2. Sheep are slow to learn.
3. Sheep are unattractive.
4. Sheep are demanding.
5. Sheep are stubborn.
6. Sheep are strong.
7. Sheep are straying.
8. Sheep are unpredictable.
9. Sheep are copycats.
10. Sheep are restless.
11. Sheep are dependent.
12. Sheep are the same everywhere.[3]

People who try (for reasons beyond me) to keep sheep as indoor pets wind up outfitting them with giant diapers because they're impossible to house-train. They poop early, often, and everywhere. And while they can be taught to do a few tricks, they're easily distracted and will walk obliviously into oncoming traffic if given the chance.

I don't think Jesus was trying to insult his followers when he called them sheep. The context of passages like Matthew 9:36 and John 10 suggests he often used it as an endearing term. But when he said God's people were like sheep without a shepherd, he implied their propensity to simply go their own way.

The practical ramification for those who work in the church—an organization populated entirely by sheep—is that there will always be a steady flow of those who wander away. In a church plant, that means exits for impulsive, unprovoked, and irrational reasons. The back door will remain well-used, no matter how many barriers you erect, how compelling your preaching is, or how delicious your free coffee tastes.

Few of us were given the heads-up that our church plant would see far more people come and leave than come and stay. When it happens, general consensus suggests spreading as many nets to retain found fish as to catch lost ones. The degree to which we concur will go a long way toward determining how angry we'll be as we walk around, how much patience we'll show, and how hopeful and encouraged we'll feel as we try to lead a flock.

So allow me to cut you loose from that heavy load and give you the most freeing advice I can offer: Don't. Chase. Christians.

JESUS DIDN'T CHASE DROPOUTS, AND NEITHER SHOULD YOU

Let me clarify. I'm not talking about refusing to build an environment where believers love one another. And I'm not suggesting you avoid addressing drift or confronting sin. A foundational trait of true agape community is that we're our brother's keepers.

We move courageously toward each other in the grace and truth of God's love. When someone stumbles, we rush to pick them up. If they drift, we erect relational guardrails to keep them from veering off the life-giving road of obedience and holiness. If we sense them pulling away, those in community with them pursue their heart to keep it from growing hard. Those who suddenly bail out for reasons such as these certainly warrant love-in-action responses from caring brothers and sisters committed to keeping one another on track.

But Jesus didn't seem concerned about creating mechanisms merely to keep his regular attendees coming back. In fact, there's not a single recorded incident in Scripture where Jesus went after someone who walked away from him and attempted to convince him or her not to.

When the wealthy young businessman in Matthew 19 declined Jesus' invitation to follow—deciding his financial portfolio superseded his commitment to God's kingdom—Jesus didn't set up another meeting to try to persuade him otherwise. He didn't alter his program or priorities to accommodate the man's schedule or fit his lifestyle. He let him walk.

When the crowds heard Jesus' hard words and complained they didn't like them, he declared, "No one can come to me unless the Father has enabled them" (John 6:65). Imagine his church planting review board's reaction if they'd heard what happened next: "From this time many of his disciples turned back and no longer followed him" (John 6:66). But Jesus didn't make a move to stop them. No appeals. No exit interviews. No "let's find a way to help you connect better" meetings. Not only did he let them go, but he pushed the back door farther open for the twelve in his core group. "You do not want to leave too, do you?" he asked them (John 6:67). Jesus grieved over the lost (Matthew 23:37), but he never chased dropouts. Ever.

Wait a minute, you say. What about Matthew 18? Jesus clearly talked about leaving the ninety-nine sheep to seek out the one lost lamb. He stated emphatically how he came to *seek* and save that which was lost (Luke 19:10).

Yes, and that's the whole point. Reaching lost ones with the gospel message should consume our attention. The Great Commission is a mandate to leave our comforts and give chase to those who haven't yet heard the gospel message. They're the ones we pursue.

But once he found them, Jesus made it very clear to the sheep where he was going. He invited them to follow, and then he let them decide whether to come along. He never turned back to try to change their minds if they declined.

INVITATIONS, NOT PLEADINGS

Jesus presented a gospel of scandalous grace, free from condition or demand. He poured out an extravagant, cleansing love, ready to drench anyone who would simply stand beneath its flow. It's the best news the world has ever been offered.

But he made sure his audience understood that the new life to which he called them would be a radically altered one. They would be invited to full repentance of their poisoned past ways. They would be remade into a new creation—one that sacrifices self and dons servant's attire. He made it clear he would ask them for a loyalty requiring abandonment of all rivals, a fully surrendered life that would be infinitely freer and far better, but one that meant death to self.

Jesus said his would be a "light" burden (Matthew 11:30), but he still called it a burden, not a vacation. He offered an "easy" yoke, but it was still an instrument of plowing. He offered "joy," but it was a joy in the midst of promised suffering. He packaged all of that into an invitation: Follow me.

Jesus urged people to weigh the cost of following him and made sure they knew the price was very high. This exchange in Luke 14 certainly doesn't sound like someone worried about closing the back door:

> Large crowds were traveling with Jesus, and turning to them he said: "If anyone comes to me and does not hate father and mother, wife and children, brothers and sisters—yes, even their own life—such a person cannot be my disciple. And whoever does not carry their cross and follow me cannot be my disciple.
>
> "Suppose one of you wants to build a tower. Won't you first sit down and estimate the cost to see if you have enough money to complete it? For if you lay the foundation and are not able to finish it, everyone who sees it will ridicule you, saying, 'This person began to build and wasn't able to finish.'

"Or suppose a king is about to go to war against another king. Won't he first sit down and consider whether he is able with ten thousand men to oppose the one coming against him with twenty thousand? If he is not able, he will send a delegation while the other is still a long way off and will ask for terms of peace. In the same way, those of you who do not give up everything you have cannot be my disciples."

LUKE 14:25–33

Even when someone presented a seemingly reasonable condition for continued involvement—taking some time away to be with his ailing father until he died—Jesus didn't offer appeasements. "Follow me now," he said. "Let the spiritually dead bury their own dead" (Matthew 8:22 NLT). When Peter asked what benefit John would receive for following, Jesus answered abruptly, "What is that to you? You must follow me" (John 21:22).

OPEN DOORS AND REGULAR INVITATIONS

It may sound cold to suggest we simply let people drop out without trying to understand why or without exploring whether there's something we can do to help them. But we're not talking about ignoring complaints or hardening our hearts toward those who may have legitimate needs. It's about respecting people's choices and refusing to be held hostage to fear.

Herm Edwards, who was a head coach in the National Football League for eight seasons, famously ranted that only one incentive should drive in-game decisions: "You play to win the game."[4] In football, a "prevent defense" is used to protect late leads, but it's often said the only thing it does is prevent victory. We play far differently when we are boldly trying to win rather than when we are cravenly attempting not to lose. Preventing the loss of people should never become our primary goal. We must always "play to win the game."

There's a way to lead those who come your way that blends freedom with responsibility.

1. Keep both doors wide open. Don't be afraid to let people know the exit door is open to them. If Christ is Lord of his church, and if following him comes at a cost, we may as well not hide that fact. We don't need to goad people to leave, but we certainly don't want to be guilty of becoming enslaved to the fear that they might. Never stop clarifying the cost of following Jesus. If people accuse us of making them uncomfortable, perhaps they've begun to grasp the true picture of what Jesus meant when he said, "But small is the gate and narrow the road that leads to life, and only a few find it" (Matthew 7:14).

At the same time, pour your efforts into the front door—not only attracting new people into public services, but opening the door of exposure to the gospel through intentional endeavors dedicated to reaching into the darkest corners of the community, serving the needy, and building bridges with those who have never heard. Our first and best energies should always be reserved for that pursuit. Go out searching for the one lost lamb. That chase is always on.

2. Pay attention to the sheep. Not chasing Christians doesn't mean ignoring them. Good shepherds, we're told, know the state of their flocks (Proverbs 27:23). Make sure the legitimate connections to which you're inviting people stay compelling and effective. Monitor the elements that keep people healthy, and if some are deficient, address them. To borrow from C. S. Lewis, invite those present to "come further in" and "further up" to the life God has designed for them in *ekklesia*.[5]

Only don't allow the sheep to dictate how they should be shepherded. A wise shepherd doesn't change direction because the sheep bleat loudly that they want to see what's "over there." He doesn't stop guiding them forward because the sheep demand he bring a certain kind of grass to them where they lie. He leads them. He ensures their safety. He directs them to the best locations for food, water, and exercise. He shears them when they need it, not when they demand it.

3. Make invitations, then let them choose. Luke 9 records a powerful statement about the path on which Jesus led his followers. Knowing full well what lay ahead for them, "As the time approached for him to be taken up to heaven, Jesus resolutely set out for Jerusalem" (Luke 9:51). *Resolutely*. Jesus carried a courageous determination to move forward on his Father's path, regardless of how difficult the road would become.

It's a pattern well worth following. Set the course, invite people onto it, and then respect their decisions to go with you or not, fully expecting that many won't. You may think you shouldn't risk leading your people into difficult trails because you need as many as you can to establish critical mass. But what you and they both need more is to resolutely set out on the kingdom road together.

CHAPTER 6

THE TRUTH ABOUT "LOTTERY WINNERS"

<u>or</u>

Fast Growth May Be Suspect Growth

I stopped going to church planter conferences. Gave it up altogether.

For a long time, I wouldn't admit the real reason—it was too self-incriminating. Someone would ask whether I was planning to attend such-and-such a conference—maybe one I'd been to a half dozen years in a row—and I'd make up excuses. I had coaching responsibilities for my daughter's soccer team; the schedule conflicted with a church event; I had some laundry to do.

But the real reason was that they sucked the life out of me. I didn't want to admit that, because it said more about me than it did about the conference itself. I just couldn't get past the parade of celebrity success stories, and the way they affected me.

The same pattern would repeat every time. An all-star lineup of gurus and up-and-comers served as keynote speakers. These were guys featured in the articles naming the most influential leaders under forty, or even thirty. Their churches had made *Outreach* magazine's list of fastest-growing or largest in the country. They'd regale us with reports of innovative feats being accomplished for the kingdom, the incredible impact God was making through their church plants . . . and could make through ours.

The stories were intended to inspire us. Except they didn't. At least not me.

Instead I cringed and ached. I felt part of myself withdraw into a dark place of envy, anger, and isolated self-loathing, because the tales they told were what I'd always envisioned would, or at least could, happen to me. I was out there grinding, praying with all the fervency I could muster, stepping out in faith, believing that God wanted my efforts to succeed. But the results were absolutely nothing like what I was hearing. There wasn't a single moment of my church planting experience that remotely resembled what was being described and presented to me.

And though disclaimers were always made—"Your results may vary"—the message was loud and clear: This is what gets noticed. This is what gets celebrated. This can be your story too.

But it wasn't. Which meant something was wrong, either with my strategy or my abilities or my faith or . . . me. And now I wasn't just inadequate; I was a horrible person. Because I couldn't even rejoice in the salvation of countless souls and the success of my teammates. Rather than celebrating the advance of the cause I absolutely believed I was part of, I was resentful it was happening.

What kind of Christian leader does that? A poser, that's what. So I'd feel envious of someone else's success, and then I'd feel overwhelming shame for feeling the envy. I should be stronger than that; I should be better than that. Who could possibly want to follow me if they knew what I was really like?

THE LOTTERY WINNERS

A small number of church planters experience a phenomenon that results in invitations to present at the conferences and seminars, or even to start one of their own. The stories follow a familiar pattern.

From humble beginnings they suddenly accelerate into explosive, rampaging growth. They hardly know what's happening and have trouble keeping up, but God keeps bringing people. Their launch service far exceeds projections. They blow through the two hundred barrier, the five hundred barrier, the one thousand barrier. They run out of space and explanations. They make some mistakes along the way but learn amazing lessons about the way the gospel advances when everyday people simply believe and move forward in God's name.

They are what I call the "lottery winners"—church plants that experience tremendous, almost instantaneous, odds-defying expansion. Like thousands of others, they played their numbers and bought their ticket, but theirs became the one-in-a-million chosen for a windfall.

When someone wins a traditional lottery, it's thrilling and awe-inspiring. There are pats on the back, giant-check presentations, and radio interviews with reporters asking how it feels to be a millionaire, where they bought the ticket, and what they're going to do first with the winnings. Distant relatives show up to congratulate the ticket holder (and position themselves to share in the bounty), and a buzz takes over the entire town. Everybody loves a rags-to-riches story, and we're fascinated when it happens overnight to someone right in front of us.

When a church plant hits the lottery, something similar takes place. The one at the center of the effort is celebrated, elevated, and thrust into the spotlight. Everyone wants to hear from them. How did it happen? What did they do? What advice would they give to others? And above all, what was the secret behind those results?

The winning church plant ticket holder, if he has any depth of character, recognizes he has very little answer for any of that. There's genuine surprise and shock at what's happened. He responds to the questions as best he can, but he's sincere in his humility—at least at first—when he gives all glory to God and says they're just trying to keep up with what God is doing at their place.

Nonetheless, he's offered book deals, podcast interview requests, and board positions. And he's invited to the next big conference to share his insights so the rest of the church planting world can be inspired and glean wisdom from his experience.

It makes sense. Burgeoning investors want to hear from Warren Buffet. Entrepreneurs want to hear from Jeff Bezos. Aspiring athletes want to hear from Tom Brady. Why wouldn't we put those with the most successful ministries on stage to inspire other church planters?

SAYING ONE THING, COMMUNICATING ANOTHER

When the lottery winners are elevated to the highest platforms, it's said to be for inspiration and education—a motivation to dream big and aim high. But what the guys in the trenches often hear is another set of messages.

1. **This represents the epitome of your profession.** "What you celebrate, you become." It's a favorite phrase in church planting circles. Nothing communicates a higher level of celebration than being handed the spotlight to teach one's peers. When that spotlight is consistently given to those who experienced triple-digit percentage growth and headline-making impact, it presents them as the top echelon of church planting, the height of what we should aspire to become.

2. **These people have discovered secrets the rest of us need to learn.** We live in a cause-and-effect world, conditioned to reverse-engineer any superior outcome to learn exactly how it

was produced. Something distinguishes those who experience exceptional, accelerated growth. They either intrinsically knew or stumbled onto a difference-making secret. If we can isolate it, learn it, and implement it, we can replicate it.

3. **You can be next.** Multilevel marketing companies have perfected the art of presenting motivational examples at their conventions. When Mary Kay Cosmetics invites its "Grand Achiever" level consultants on stage at annual meetings and presents them with their pink cars, they ignite a passion within the newly minted salesperson in the audience with a prevailing thought: someday, this could be you. Highlight the exceptional, and you motivate imitation.

I now live in one of Southern California's best-known surfing communities. Everywhere you walk along the coastline, dozens of surfers sit patiently on their boards, watching the horizon. They're all hoping for the same thing—to be the one who catches the next big wave. There's a surfing museum not far from us, and its walls are filled with pictures celebrating the best surfers in history, riding some of the largest waves ever caught. Those pictures embed the ultimate goal into every young grommet who sees them—to someday catch and ride the ultimate wave, as big as the ones depicted for them.

When the pictures posted on the walls of our church planting circles are of those who have caught the largest waves, they communicate a clear message: You should be catching those waves. You can make that story your story.

But it's not going to be my story. It's not going to be yours. We've been presented a fantasy.

(NO) HARM, (NO) FOUL

While I'm confident Christian book publishers and church planting conference producers mean no harm by reserving the largest platform for the lottery winners, harm can nonetheless be done. The intention may be to inspire, equip, and motivate, but two significant negative effects can result. Amazingly, both can happen simultaneously within the same person.

Amplified Disappointment

When consistently superlative results are presented as our model—when exponential growth is portrayed as attainable and reasonable—we're set up for intense disappointment after our situation produces merely typical results. What would otherwise have been viewed as healthy and normative now appears deeply subpar compared to the benchmark we've been given.

I'm a lifelong New York Mets and New York Jets fan, which means one thing: I have suffered greatly. When your fan heritage has been marked not just by losing, but losing in the most excruciatingly painful ways possible, the rare winning season or playoff appearance feels like momentary nirvana. I'm stunned any time it happens, and never, ever gloat if it does. I know better. I'm aware it's an aberration—that I'll most likely be right back to where I've always been all too soon. I can enjoy the moment, but I'd be a fool to expect or demand that it be the norm.

I experienced the polar opposite side of fandom when we moved to Columbus, Ohio. I entered Ohio State Buckeye football territory and encountered a fan base so conditioned to winning, to competing for Big Ten and national championships nearly every year, that I couldn't begin to relate to the expectation. When the team did have a down year or, for that matter, a down game, it was as if someone had just shot everyone's puppy. People didn't know how to cope. Literally half our congregation wouldn't show up for church on days after losses. Amplified expectation creates devastating disappointment.

I mentioned in the introduction that I invited other area church planters to find an honest, safe group of guys who could relate to the challenges and struggles we all face. In those days, the Willow Creek Association produced a monthly newsletter for its members, and each edition featured an article on the back cover about a member church. They consistently told the success stories—glowing reports of amazing growth from an association church. I confessed to the group that, odious as it might sound, reading those stories had the effect of hooking up a hose to my soul and draining me dry.

Instantly, just about everyone in the room jumped in to admit the exact same reaction.

Empowered by at least not feeling like the only disease carrier out there, we began to compare notes and to question the way such stories were paraded on stage and written about in the books and magazines. We became more and more convinced those articles must have been the brainchild of people who had never actually planted a church and who therefore had no idea of the effect it was having on those of us who read them.

My good friend Phil decided to do something about it, and he wrote a letter to the editors of the Willow Creek newsletter. He explained how some of us who plant churches weren't being inspired but demoralized every time we heard another story. To the WCA's credit, they replied to Phil's letter with a very sympathetic, affirming tone. They thanked him for his honesty, and with his permission they published his letter anonymously, with an apology to others who might have been similarly affected. The response was overwhelming. An avalanche of planters and pastors echoed the same reaction. In time, the WCA removed those stories from the publication altogether.

Maybe we should have been mature enough to react more positively to those articles, but the fact is we all have feet of clay and, until we reach a level of maturity few of us have yet attained, this is how it tends to affect real people.

Lemmings and Groupies

The second effect appears to come from the opposite end of the spectrum. But some of the same people who inwardly die a little every time they're presented with grand tales of adventure also stuff their backpacks with every method, technique, and principle they hear in the hope that this time it will prove to be the catalyst for their own exponential growth.

We want to know exactly what the lottery winners did, and the order in which they did it. What was different about the team they assembled? What marketing tools did they develop? What sermon series did they preach? What music did they play? What graphics did they use in their projections?

We adopt the same children's curriculum, replicate the organizational chart, and preach with the same style and passion. One church I consulted with was so committed to following the lead of an explosive-growth megachurch that they literally matched the fabric the megachurch had used to upholster their auditorium seats.

The throng takes copious notes and then returns home to enact the same steps in the same order, hoping for the same results.

LIVING IN REALITY

Highlighting the one-in-a-million church planters provides some amazing stories that remind us how God still occasionally does earthshaking things. But it might be worthwhile for someone to pull back the curtain just a bit and reveal three things even the lottery winners know to be true.

1. Someone wins the lottery, but no one wins the lottery. *Fortune* magazine published a list of things more likely to happen to a person than winning a Powerball lottery. They include being hit by a meteorite, drowning in a Grand Canyon flash flood, and sinking three consecutive hole in ones on the golf course.[1]

While it's true that *somebody* wins the lottery, any meaningful statistical measurement tells us essentially no one wins the lottery; at least no one you know, and most assuredly not you. Astounding stories of church plants that mushroom overnight and become the stuff of legend are no more real-life attainable than starting a company that becomes Google or Amazon. It happens, but rarely enough that it should never be presented as an attainable goal. To do so is to be irresponsible to the countless entrepreneurs who deserve better than to be measured by an unattainable standard.

2. Duplicate results can never be reproduced by the same method. Even long-term lottery players, who consistently pay the "tax on people who are bad at math," know better than to think they can find a past winner, play the exact same numbers, and expect them to produce another winner.

Business and ministry parallel each other in a number of ways, but there is one paramount way in which they are fundamentally different. Business follows fairly consistent patterns of effective methodology and predictable customer behavior. As discussed in chapter 2, the church, because it trades in a commodity that is spiritual at its root, does not advance via corporeal systems. As Scripture makes abundantly clear, the catalytic part of life change lies completely outside the capacities of human effort (1 Corinthians 3:7).

Let me put it another way. We don't create wind; we only erect wind turbines. Unless the wind blows, our turbines do nothing but pepper the landscape like so many metal toothpicks. We're utterly dependent on a force outside ourselves to supply the energy. When a church experiences profound impact and responsiveness, it may be tempting to study the placement of the wind farm, replicate the pattern, and hope to produce the same results elsewhere. But wind formation pays no heed to our turbine arrays. Humbling as it is to admit, the variables we have under our control to bring about exponential growth equal those capable of producing wind—zero.

3. **Fast growth may be suspect growth.** This brings us to the next dirty little secret of the church planting world and of church growth as a whole: Fast growth may be suspect growth. In God's great design for creation, healthy things grow. But his clear pattern is for growth to happen slowly, through sustained investment. When anything expands too quickly—or instantaneously—it points to suspicious causes and usually results in less-than-healthy outcomes.

Physically, a healthy young person grows, but if one grows too quickly, something is wrong. I had a middle school friend who absolutely swore he'd discovered a way he could make himself two inches taller overnight, anytime he wanted. It involved drinking some sort of concoction and stretching his limbs a certain way as he fell asleep. Yeah, he was kind of weird . . . although he *was* a good four inches taller than me, so maybe he was onto something.

When a child grows abnormally fast, it is a marker for diseases such as Sotos syndrome, where fast growth indicates hormonal imbalance and can be accompanied by disorders like autism; delayed motor, cognitive, and social development; and speech impairments.[2]

Financial growth follows the same created pattern. Investments that return a dividend far outpacing the market average generally belie a Madoff-type pyramid scheme or insider trading. Scripture underscores the pursuit of slow growth monetarily in the wisdom of Proverbs 13:11 (NLT): "Wealth from get-rich-quick schemes quickly disappears; wealth from hard work grows over time."

As we'll see further in the next chapter, spiritual transformation mirrors the created order of slow, sustained growth. Jesus said to beware of fast growth in response to the gospel; it almost certainly will prove rootless (Matthew 13:5–6, 20–21). History records a scant few incidents where record numbers of true, supernaturally fueled conversions occurred in a short amount of time. Acts 2 is one of them. But in almost every case of fast numeric church growth, closer scrutiny reveals it to be artificial.

It's almost all transfer growth.

In a 2015 *Christian Post* article, Greg Laurie cites David Dunlap's estimate that up to 80 percent of all growth in churches comes from transfers rather than conversions.[3] Mike Breen estimated that number to be even higher. He wrote in *Mission Frontiers* magazine, "Ninety-six percent of church growth is due to transfer growth and not churches striking into the heart of our enemy's territory. We'll consider it a win because we have the new service or program that is growing . . . but that growth is mainly from people coming from other churches. That's not a win! That's a staggering loss."[4]

Joel Rainey's extensive doctoral research at the Southern Baptist Theological Seminary concluded that churches focused on reaching the unchurched tend to grow more slowly than those who don't.[5]

Practically every explosive-growth church I've studied firsthand has been the recipient of another significant factor in its community that contributed dramatically to the influx. In one, an existing large church not far away made a major theological shift, and hundreds of exiles herded together toward the new church. In another, a lead pastor's moral failure resulted in huge numbers gravitating to a church that was starting down the road. On multiple occasions, an influx of new homes and residents in an area coincided with the opening of a church plant there, bringing in displaced believers looking for a new base.

To be fair, many of those churches also saw solid first-time conversions—people repenting of sin and turning to Christ in life-altering decisions of surrender. The gospel is still changing lives.

But the largest waves were made up of transfers who already knew Christ. The faster the growth, the more likely the church grew as a receptor of reshuffled sheep rather than through first-time converts.

It's time to rethink who we elevate as church planting role models and motivational examples. How can we spare ourselves the shame of inferior comparison to unrealistic standards? How do we hang different pictures on our walls?

STOP SPOTLIGHTING LOTTERY WINNERS

We can start by making a conscious shift in the criteria used for deciding who we put on stage at our gatherings and who we sign to book deals.

We don't need the latest trendsetter explaining how their creative missional activity or the newest innovations in lighting and tech can take us from the poor saps we are to the movers and shakers we were intended to be. Listen to what Eugene Peterson, whose church never landed on the "100 fastest-growing" lists, had to say in his memoir *The Pastor*: "I was astonished to learn in one of these best-selling books [on church life] that the size of my church parking lot had far more to do with how things fared in my congregation than my choice of texts in preaching. I was being lied to and I knew it."[6]

Reflecting on the models posited for modern-day pastors, he wrote, "The vocation of pastor has been replaced by the strategies of religious entrepreneurs with business plans. Any kind of continuity with pastors in times past is virtually nonexistent."[7]

If you're a church planter fixated on the record-setting, fast-growth examples offered as inspiration to achieve great things, know that when you feel inadequate or compulsive in response, you're not abnormal. When you're told . . .

- they have, know, or do something you're missing—they don't.
- their story is one you should attempt to emulate—it isn't.
- they're blessed and anointed in ways you aren't but should be—they're not.
- you can be the next lottery winner, if you only aspire to it, work toward it, and trust God to bring it—you won't.

Conference sponsors may contend, "But we don't do that. We feature a broad spectrum of pastors, leaders, and organizations who don't boast large numbers or fast growth. We make it clear that leaders working in smaller churches are just as valuable, just as wise, and just as blessed as those whose churches happened to grow fast and large." There's one simple test to determine whether that's true: Who is given the main stage? Answer that, and you'll know what is most highly valued and affirmed.

But . . . but . . . but . . . people won't come to a conference featuring presenters they've never heard of. Then why are we doing the conference? If the answer is, "To inspire leaders," the next question becomes, "Inspire them to what?" To produce something over which they have no control? To compare their results to outcomes only God determines?

I applaud the efforts of veteran pastors like J. R. Briggs, who recognized this problem and convened the first-of-its-kind Epic Fail Pastors Conference in 2011.[8] It represented a courageous honesty to say that feeling like a failure is an extremely common occurrence among church planters and pastors. It also recognized the value of building community and sharing ideas among those who are experiencing kingdom work the way it almost always goes.

Briggs has established a means by which similar gatherings can continue through regional events, but sadly, very few actually happen. We apparently prefer to keep buying lottery tickets.

Let's turn the spotlight off the exceptions and aberrations. Let's stop promoting the lottery.

CHANGING PODCAST SUBSCRIPTIONS

Instead, let's elevate, celebrate, and make more room on the main platform for the long-term, faithful veterans with a reputation for retaining healthy environments and staying on task. A quiet army of persevering servants has endured through the kind of unsplashy, incremental growth we'll examine in the next chapter. Theirs are the stories we're most likely to emulate if we're doing it right. They're the ones whose pattern we'd do best to follow. Let's put them on stage and sit at their feet for a while.

Gene Edwards has been that kind of voice. An exceptional writer and thinker, he pastored inauspicious churches that never set any attendance records or made headlines. He's never written how-to articles revealing "the six secrets to explosive growth." Instead he's penned works like *The Prisoner in the Third Cell, The Divine Romance,* and the book I've recommended to others in ministry more often than any other with the exception of the Bible itself—*A Tale of Three Kings.*

In it, Edwards wrote this about what to look for in our influencers: "What does this world need: gifted men and women, outwardly empowered? Or individuals who are broken, inwardly transformed?"[9] If we seek out the successful, if we pray for the powerful, he said, "those prayers sound powerful, sincere, godly, and without ulterior motive. Hidden under such prayer and fervor, however, are ambition, a craving for fame, the desire to be considered a spiritual giant. The person who prays such a prayer may not even know it, but dark motives and desires are in his heart . . . in *your* heart."[10]

To whom do you grant the platform as your example and

inspiration for planting your visionary church? Whose blogs do you read and podcasts do you subscribe to? Which speaker entices you to sign up for the conference? What church's patterns do you seek to emulate or learn from?

Explosive growth in any gospel endeavor is worth celebrating, and those leading fast-growing churches are tremendous teammates in the kingdom's advance. But when we share center stage with those who—to borrow a phrase from Eugene Peterson (and Friedrich Nietzsche)—walk "a long obedience in the same direction," we'll free ourselves from the debilitating discouragement that descends when we inevitably don't hit the lottery ourselves. And we'll revel more fully in the vibrant stories of life transformation, which occur one at a time, at a pace we'll talk about next, over a lifetime of sustained investment.

RETURNING TO THE CONFERENCES

I've come to the place where I can praise God with a growing measure of authentic joy when I hear of a church plant that erupted into prominence. I can take in an occasional conference, because I've gotten better at screening out implications that the success stories are sourced in a specific individual or a superior methodology. They literally could happen to anyone who is trying to reach lost people. Anyone. It's worth praising God for.

If you can do that, go to the conference. Take your team. Be inspired. Glean from the helpful resources and "best practices" shared. Then return home free from the pressure to recreate anything you've just seen.

Today I can freely delight in a spectacular sunset, because I know I carry away no responsibility to replicate it. I can simply watch appreciatively the next time one shows up.

CHAPTER 7

THE TRUTH ABOUT PACE

or

It's No Fun Watching Dough Rise

Before it became politically incorrect to tease anyone anywhere about anything, a song poked fun at Toledo, Ohio, for being a place where nothing ever happens. "Saturday Night in Toledo, Ohio," it said, "is like being nowhere at all"—a place where dazzling entertainment consists of going to "visit the bakery and watch the buns rise."[1]

There's nothing exciting about watching dough rise. But when Jesus described how God's kingdom advances, that was one of the word pictures he chose. "The kingdom of heaven," he said, "is like yeast that a woman took and mixed into about sixty pounds of flour until it worked all through the dough" (Matthew 13:33). Effective . . . but slow. You don't hear a lot of sermons on that one. There are no pyrotechnics, no walking on water, no three thousand salvations at one Pentecostal rally. It sure isn't something you buy tickets to watch.

But God's timing and pace are illustrated in similar terms throughout the New Testament. James likened waiting for Jesus to establish his kingdom to a farmer "patiently waiting for the autumn and spring rains" (James 5:7). Peter talked about the time until Christ's return being marked in units of measure utterly different from ours: "With the Lord . . . a thousand years are like a day," he wrote (2 Peter 3:8). There's nothing remotely fast in those descriptions.

So it's curious how modern church planting has put so much emphasis on ways to increase the speed with which we make progress. There's no shortage of books, articles, and seminars uncovering the secrets to accelerating the pace of moving people from "spiritually disinterested" to "reproducing disciple."

In the last chapter, we considered how celebrating and chasing fast growth is a misguided pursuit, how fast growth may be suspect growth. Fine, we say. We don't much like it, but we can get used to the idea that explosive growth isn't common and may not be trustworthy. We can ratchet down our expectations and cool our jets.

But there's still more to the equation. God doesn't just caution against fast change; he introduces a kingdom-advancement pace that shocks us by moving decidedly slower than even our adjusted expectations.

GOD'S "SLOW" IS SLOWER THAN OUR "SLOW"

Isaiah 55:9 is well-known for establishing God's ways as higher than our ways, and his thoughts as higher than our thoughts. But another of his distinguishing features reveals itself when we enact pioneering ministry in his name: God's "slow" is slower than our "slow."

Like, really slow. Like, "so slow you can't tell anything's happening" slow. God has seldom been accused of acting too quickly, but he's been railed against plenty of times for moving at a snail's pace. "How long, Lord, how long?" the psalmist bemoaned (Psalms 6:3; 13:1). The psalms of lament are full of frustrated complaints asking God what's taking so long. Four hundred years of slavery before emancipation? Forty years of nomadic circle spinning before entering the Promised Land? Seventy years of oppression before returning from exile? Couldn't he get on with it already?

Nothing changed when Jesus arrived. Charles Spurgeon wrote, "Our Lord Jesus Christ was never in a hurry. It is marvellous to contemplate the leisure of the greatest Worker who ever lived. He always moved along with a holy calm and quiet dignity, and he therefore did everything well."[2]

That makes it sound all noble and distinguished. But it drove Jesus' followers up the wall. Martha's consternation was only thinly veiled when she asked Jesus why he took his sweet time getting to Lazarus, when he knew his friend was near death. "If you had been here," she complained, "my brother would not have died" (John 11:21).

The disciples couldn't for the life of them fathom why Jesus didn't install his kingdom immediately. More than once, they expected him to ascend the throne on the spot. When Jesus entered Jerusalem, the crowds formed a parade route to welcome the rebel king, assuming the coronation would fall on that week's schedule (Luke 19:11). After Jesus rose from the dead, the question came again, "Are you at this time going to restore the kingdom?" (Acts 1:6).

Each time they asked and the answer came back, "Not yet," everyone kind of cocked their heads to the side like a dog perplexed that his master would make him wait for a treat.

THE THREE MPH GOD

Japanese theologian Kosuke Koyama referred to this trait of unhurriedness as the "three mile an hour God," adducing the casual pace Jesus most likely walked.[3] God *says* he wants his cause to advance, but he never seems to be in a rush to make it happen, even when it comes to enacting his grand plan for redemption. He's only ever shown himself to move at three speeds: slow, slower, and slowest.

And that makes no sense to us whatsoever.

Our reasoning goes like this. We know these incontrovertible truths:

1. **People are lost and need rescue.** Every single moment since paradise was lost in the garden has pointed toward one overarching objective—to break the ensuing curse of death and restore the capstone of God's creation (human beings) to their intended position.

2. **God is focused and relentless.** The delivery and embrace of redemption's good news stands as the single most significant endeavor on earth. The entirety of the human story revolves around the making and redeeming of God's kingdom.

3. **Time is short.** More than two thousand years ago, Jesus said time was short. Work now, he said, because the day is soon coming when the opportunity to work will be over (John 9:4). Paul declared with a sense of urgency, "Now is the day of salvation" (2 Corinthians 6:2).

If all that is true, wouldn't God want to act with lightning speed to bring about change as quickly as humanly (or even divinely) possible? What gives?

When we plant a church—the expressed purpose of which is to accomplish God's singular highest mission—we pray for, work toward, expect, and *need* him to bring progress to our efforts at a reasonable pace. Instead, everything seems to happen in slow motion. Days, weeks, and even months pass without a single praiseworthy event occurring. The inertia exasperates us.

It also does something else. It forces us to recalibrate our internal speed gauges to accommodate a couple of intrinsic "God values." And like it or not, these values virtually guarantee that the kingdom pace will move much more slowly than we expect.

TRANSFORMATION OVER CONVERSION

In my early church circles, "evangelism" was known by one name—"door-to-door witnessing." Armed with our trusty fake survey forms, we'd step out courageously, knock on strangers' doors, and invite folks to answer a few questions (the results of which were never compiled) in hopes of sharing the gospel and closing the sale on the spot. We'd gather afterward to report how many people prayed with us to receive Christ, like gunslingers showing off notches for kills on our holsters.

What was never discussed, though, was how many of those people would be walking with Jesus a year or two later. We never knew—and, frankly, didn't much care—how many of them ever reoriented their lives to know him deeply, connect with others in his Name, or repent from debilitating sin. We didn't have time for all that; we just wanted to see "decisions" for Christ. Conversions.

But God has never been about hit-and-run conversions. What he's after is lasting transformation. N. T. Wright addresses this distinction in *After You Believe*:

> Many Christians have so emphasized the need for conver-
> sion, for the opening act of faith and commitment, for the
> initial statement of that faith ("believing that Jesus died for
> me" or whatever), that they have a big gap in their vision of

what being a Christian is all about. It's as though they were standing on one side of a deep, wide river, looking across to the further bank. On *this* bank you declare your faith. On the *opposite* bank is the ultimate result—final salvation itself. But what are people supposed to do in the meantime? Simply stand here and wait? Is there no bridge between the two? What does this say about faith itself? If we're not careful . . . this opening act of belief can become "simply a matter of assent to a proposition (Jesus is Son of God, etc.), with no need for transformation."[4]

We may as well substitute "church planters" or "church planting organizations" for "Christians" in his first sentence. Conversions appeal to us because they represent quick, measurable, tangible progress that gives us the sensation of movement. Transformation—the utter reshaping of a person's heart and character—is less obvious and only evidences itself over protracted time.

When we returned from our cold-turkey witnessing, we would produce names of people who had made verbal confessions that their lives were forever changed. Conversion calls that "mission accomplished." Transformation says, "Time will tell."

Paul's greatest focus, prayers, and even pain (which he likened to childbirth—a risky analogy to invoke with mothers in the audience) were centered around one predominant goal: "until Christ is formed in you" (Galatians 4:19). Romans 8:29 speaks of God's objective for us to be "conformed to the image of his Son." Second Corinthians 3:18 reads, "We are being transformed into [Christ's] image." Each of these passages uses verbs derived from the same Greek root word, transliterated *morph*. This points to a fundamental change from one entity into another, over time. God's purpose is to utterly change the essence of a person. This kind of transformation simply cannot be rushed.

SUBSTANCE OVER SPEED

In God's economy, he introduces something he values more than speed—substance. And in his design for real, lasting transformation within the human heart, the second part of the principle introduced in the previous chapter can be seen: *Fast growth may be suspect growth. Slow growth is substantive growth.*

God isn't interested in statistics or "decisions." He desires alteration at the core, on a cellular level. "You desire truth in the inward parts," David wrote (Psalm 51:6 NKJV). That occurs slowly, incrementally, through repeated influence. It proceeds from a combination of elements that cannot be condensed or substituted. The equation is simple and universal:

Sustained Investment + Incremental Progress + Time = Substantive Growth

That equation holds true in just about every realm of created life:

- *Relationships* take time to deepen and grow roots that will carry them through the inevitable turbulent times.
- *Wealth* is best accumulated through consistent investment, compounding interest, and time.
- *Crops* can't be rushed if they're going to produce the fullest harvest. They need, as we already noted James as teaching, the spring and autumn rains.

Remove any of the elements—sustained involvement, incremental progress, time—and substantive growth is stunted. There may be temporary signs of movement, but transformation only emerges when all three remain consistently present.

We're rightfully suspicious of an unfaithful spouse who suddenly declares himself a "different person," committed never to cheat again. Twelve-step groups challenge and correct any participants who hastily announce they're "over" their addiction. People who quickly lose significant weight through fad diets draw skeptical reactions when they donate their wardrobes to Goodwill and proclaim they're done with overeating. In all these scenarios, the response from a watching, street-savvy world remains the same: "We'll see."

A young couple with a boatload of marital problems began attending our church. New in their faith, they confessed deep issues of distrust and disrespect but were eager and open to God's intervention. We offered them counseling through a local Christian agency, and they set an appointment. On the eve of the first session, I received a call from the wife, who reported she and her husband had just spent a tremendously constructive weekend together. They'd experienced a breakthrough, she said, and "everything is good now." I affirmed the positive news and encouraged her that counseling would serve as a great next step. She informed me they'd canceled the appointment because they knew things were miraculously repaired, and they didn't want to harp on the negative.

Six months later, they filed for divorce. Both left the church.

There was another couple. They experienced a fiery time of infidelity and affair. I sat with them at the moment she admitted what she had denied vehemently for weeks—her inappropriate contact with another man had indeed become sexual.

What followed was an excruciatingly difficult season of mistrust, with fits of anger, moments of softening, and long hours of discussion, counseling, and hard work. Multiple times, I thought, *This is it. It's over.*

But they hung in there. They established new dynamics, tough accountability, and disciplined habits. Their marriage slowly transformed. Three years later, they had come to the place where they were able to share their story publicly, and they became an instrument to help other couples experiencing similar challenges.

Those stories epitomize the difference between fast change and substantive change. If you prefer the latter, it will come slowly and incrementally. Spiritual transformation is like fine wine, gourmet cheese, or leather. It must cure to reach its fullest potency. The process can't be rushed or accelerated. You may as well get used to it.

SLOW-COOKER LESSONS

I heard a good friend use a phrase he may or may not have coined, but which I've repeated so often I now pretty much claim it as my own: "We have five-year plans. God has thousand-year plans."

Once it dawns on us that nothing we do can hasten the slow crawl God insists on his progress taking, we can embrace some ramifications that make church planting much less sexy but that also free us to take some pressure off.

1. **Life change (and thus church planting) is slow, arduous work.** We can raise our swords and yell "attack" to take the next hill, but sometimes the army behind us is full of soldiers still on crutches from past battles, carrying others on stretchers. After a while, the excitement of starting a new church wears off like new car smell. It loses most of the exhilaration it once promised.

But being slowed by the transformation process is not an indicator of *lost* vision; it's a sign of *fulfilled* vision. This is what we asked for. We accepted the mission to rescue POWs trapped in the jungle. Once we find them, we've got to slog through the muck to bring them home. To paraphrase vintage John Mellencamp, "Oh yeah, [church planting] goes on, long after the thrill of [church planting] is gone."

It begins to make sense why Scripture so commonly calls on

leaders to exhibit patience above nearly every other virtue. We can feel Paul's resignation in 1 Thessalonians 5:14: "We urge you, brothers and sisters, warn those who are idle and disruptive, encourage the disheartened, help the weak." Then it's almost as if he throws his hands up in resignation as he declares, "Be patient with everyone."

Church planting could stand a dose of de-sensationalizing. Like private detectives and lawyers, those who actually do it for a living will tell you it's nothing like it's depicted on TV. It's mostly mundane, grind-it-out, nothing-thrilling-happened-again-today work. My colleague Scott Wagoner likes to say the vast majority of church planting comes down to "blocking and tackling." Paul's advice to the Galatians applies especially to those planting churches: "Let us not become weary in doing good, for at the proper time we will reap a harvest if we do not give up" (Galatians 6:9).

2. Leaders do well to slow themselves to match God's pace. Peter Marshall, arguably the most famous chaplain in the history of the United States Senate, once prayed at the invocation of a session, "In the name of Jesus Christ, who was never in a hurry, we pray, O God, that thou wilt slow us down, for we know that we live too fast. With all of eternity before us, make us take time to live—time to get acquainted with thee, time to enjoy thy blessings, and time to know each other."[5]

If we insist on running at a fevered clip to accomplish God's work, we'll frustrate ourselves and ruin our health at the same time. The principle of Sabbath rest deserves far more attention than I can give here, but Type A/High D/Choleric/Lion personality types universally need to take the unnatural step of slowing the truck down. Dallas Willard hammered this truth home relentlessly when addressing spiritual wholeness in leaders. For you to move toward and maintain spiritual health, he said, "You must ruthlessly eliminate hurry from your life."[6]

That means focusing on the odometer more than the speedometer. It means choosing not to force the issue but allowing the ministry to come to you instead. Workaholism is an overused term in our culture, but many church planters sacrifice their health, their family dynamic, and their perspective on its altar.

Pace doesn't equal impact. Keeping a regular, true Sabbath is something many planters abandon early in the name of entrepreneurism. It's a fatal mistake. And it doesn't make any difference anyway. When the U-Haul's engine is equipped with a governor, you can push the gas pedal through the floorboard all you want; you'll never move faster than the speed limit. Relax the pressure on the accelerator, and you'll find that the vehicle still moves at pretty much the same pace, while your anxiety level will drop significantly.

3. **Dig in for the long haul.** Couples who have been married for more than fifty years experience a level of marital satisfaction far surpassing any other group. Maybe it's just because they've given up their idealistic notions of what marriage should deliver. But more likely, it's because a depth of intimacy, trust, camaraderie, and partnership emerges only after long, continued investment in a marriage.

Sadly, most couples never get there. The 2010 United States Census revealed that only 55 percent of all couples have been married at least fifteen years. Less than 35 percent reach their twenty-fifth anniversary. And only 6 percent of marriages make it to a golden anniversary.[7] Ah, but those who do make it report unparalleled levels of joy and gratification.

The slow pace and hard work of church planting leads too many good men and women to cash in their chips prematurely. It's amazing how many church planters—and pastors in general—suddenly feel the "call of God" to move on to another church or ministry after a half dozen years, if not sooner. We don't want to admit it, but a big part of the reason is the thanklessly slow pace and lack of discernible progress.

Hear this as a call for church planters to dig in for the long haul. Yes, there are some apostolic types among us who are very much perpetual starters, uniquely designed to rally the front end of an effort and then move on to do it again. Paul the apostle was such a person. But the sustained labor in the trenches—the work of sticking with people, of helping them learn how to carry their own burdens plus one another's, of persevering through the down markets and staying in the mix until there's sufficient time to see the long-term effects—that's where the deepest joy comes.

And, as always, the result is that God gets the glory for accomplishing what has been done, in his own time, at a pace only he fully understands but that gives us a satisfaction of witnessing true, substantive transformation.

In the end, you'll find *that's* what you really wanted all along.

8

THE TRUTH ABOUT "CHURCH MULTIPLICATION MOVEMENTS"

or

You Don't Get to Be Moses

You say you want a revolution.
Well . . . we all want to change the world.

THE BEATLES[1]

One of the most-viewed videos in the history of the TED Talks is also one of its shortest. Derek Sivers's three-minute speech, "How to Start a Movement," features hilarious amateur footage of a lone, shirtless man dancing (with little discernible skill) at an outdoor concert. Oblivious to how ridiculous he looks, he keeps it up until another man joins him. The first follower waves in a few friends, and within three minutes, the crazy dance becomes a "movement." The entire crowd eventually joins "Shirtless Dancing Guy" on the hillside, frolicking to the music.[2]

Sivers noted that in the scenario, "Shirtless Dancing Guy" is the catalyst, obviously important because he needed the guts to stand out and be ridiculed. But it is the first follower who "transforms a lone nut into a leader." Then, because the act is public, as it draws more followers, momentum is established until it reaches a tipping point where everybody feels they must join in or risk being left out. And thus a movement is begun.

"WE NEED A CHURCH MULTIPLICATION MOVEMENT"

In recent years, church planters have heard a consistent challenge, not only to plant churches, but to launch a church multiplication movement. The gauntlet is regularly thrown down in books and at conventions. Don't just plant a church. And don't merely birth a church that can birth a church. Capture God's dream and create a movement.

Ed Stetzer and Warren Bird offered a tangible definition of what would qualify as such a movement in their book *Viral Churches*: "A church multiplication movement is a rapid reproduction rate of 50 percent through the third generation of churches, with new churches having 50 percent new converts. To achieve such momentum, churches would need to plant, on average, a new church every two years with each church reaching at least half its attendees from the unchurched community."[3]

Wow. That would be fantastic.

We're told we're both capable and on the cusp of making that dream a reality. That a multiplication movement is God's vision for the contemporary church in these latter days. That he is waiting to bless those who pray for it, believe it, and step out to lead toward it.

Who would question the dream of living so sold-out, so full of faith, that we ignite a generation and initiate unprecedented kingdom advance? Max Lucado wrote, "Each of us should lead a life stirring enough to start a movement."[4]

And apparently almost anyone can do it. *Chicken Soup for the Soul* author Jack Canfield is often quoted: "One individual can begin a movement that turns the tide of history. Martin Luther King in the civil rights movement, Mohandas Gandhi in India, Nelson Mandela in South Africa are examples of people standing up with courage and non-violence to bring about needed changes."[5]

Scott Goodson, author of the bestseller *Uprising*, wrote, "Today, anyone of the billions of people on the planet can start a movement that spreads like wildfire . . . Any individual around the planet, any politician, any community organizer, any artist or tech innovator and business people."[6] Simple enough. In that case, there's no excuse for those leading the greatest cause on earth not to do so.

The message is clear: You're called to do more than just birth a church. The mission is a bigger, "God-sized" mandate. God's purpose and plan is to see "multiplying churches" that launch a movement, one that penetrates the world and makes revolutionary impact in this generation for the gospel. Put simply . . .

Good	Planting a Church
Better	Planting a Reproducing Church
Best	Planting a Multiplying Church

So, if you're a church planter, you need to dream big. Shoot high. You can do more than plant a church; you can start a movement.

IF YOU'RE NOT WINNING, YOU'RE LOSING

To drive home the point, some daunting statistics are offered concerning the current condition of American churches. Eighty percent are said to be either plateaued or declining in attendance. Only 4 percent currently qualify as "reproducing"—those actively planting daughter churches. And "multiplying churches," while more common in other cultures, are nearly nonexistent in America. We're invited and challenged to take the steps necessary to move up the scale toward movement making, which is presented as God's undisputed vision.

For many of those trudging through the church planting marshlands, hearing that challenge serves to shame as much as to inspire. If my church falls into that sad-sack group of bottom rungers—plateaued or, heaven forbid, declining—we're clearly in need of radical retreading so we can somehow escape being sent to the slow learners class.

The implication, intended or not, is that anything less than "movement"-level multiplication represents a degree of failure to fulfill God's ultimate wish. Grouping existing churches so that four-fifths are defined as stagnant or declining serves as an indictment. Any fast-food franchise or retail chain showing plateaued or declining sales in 80 percent of its locations would not be long for this world.

Todd Wilson and Dave Ferguson, whose efforts cofounding Exponential have contributed as significantly to church planting's advance as any in this generation, have proposed an ambitious dream: to see the ratio of "multiplying churches" in North America increase from 4 percent to 10 percent. Count me among those who would love to see it. But even if that dream were realized, it would mean 90 percent of us will never plant a "multiplying" church. That doesn't make the 90 percent failures.

EVERYBODY WANTS TO RULE THE WORLD

Lofty as the call to become a movement maker may sound, it fails to take into consideration three realities that ensure it to be an all but untenable pursuit.

1. **Spiritual market fluctuations in the body.** It's no secret the evangelical church in America suffers from a lack of leadership and vision. But the broad-brush inference that a church experiencing plateau or decline does so for lack of these elements ignores the inevitability of what we might call "spiritual market fluctuations."

Nothing grows on a constant, "upward and to the right" chart trajectory. And that goes for the spiritual condition of any flock we ever shepherd. Oh, we *want* our people to progress consistently toward multiplication, and we steer in that direction. But we're in a battle against the age-old triumvirate of enemies—the world, the flesh, and the devil. As long as that trio is present, they'll routinely create temporary bear markets in the spiritual climate.

Just about the time we think we're making headway, some of our best people suddenly career off course. It happens in every church, but you notice it more quickly in a church plant. A small group facilitator becomes sexually involved with the wife of another man in his group. A key leader is exposed as battling a porn addiction (joining 80 percent of the men in your church). Someone you've celebrated as a trophy of grace, sober for more than ten years, relapses and checks back into rehab. These aren't contrived examples. Every one of them actually happened in our church plant.

When crises like these occur, they instantly impede your ability to spearhead expansion, much less launch a movement. They demand that you divert your attention and jump into triage mode. You attend to expanding circles of casualties that extend far beyond those at the center of the problem. You put out fires and perform major surgeries. That's the reality of trench warfare.

Then another reality follows. First responders are inevitably among those most criticized in the aftermath of disaster. FEMA should have arrived sooner. Police officers should have followed a different protocol. Medics said or did things that caused more harm than good. The haze of pain fogs the vision of where to lay blame, so first responders wind up on the receiving end because they're directly in the line of sight.

And that's you. You rush in to help but find yourself attacked for not helping faster or more effectively. You're accused of ulterior motives, taking sides, pushing too hard or not hard enough. Now you're not only dealing with the setbacks and delays the initial problem caused, but you're also exerting further time and energy defending yourself for the way you and your church responded.

All of this serves to grind any forward progress to a halt. Forget igniting a movement; you're doing well just to keep your head above water.

You're in the "plateaued/declining" 80 percent.

But that doesn't mean your church is failing its mission. On the contrary, these ugly, dirty, debilitating episodes often serve as a sign of health within a church body. God is working to expose sin, bring people to the admission of their true condition, and foster an environment of honesty and grace where people's true selves can be revealed. Some of the most significant seasons for a church are those in which deep pruning and correction take place. All of that requires that increased attention be paid to those already in the fold as opposed to moving forward to take more territory.

We say we want the church to be a spiritual hospital . . . until the ambulances start arriving. If we're spending full days treating patients—slowly nursing some back to health, performing CPR on others, and at times doing everything we can, only to see them recover enough to return to the very practices that got them sick in the first place—are those not still worthwhile days?

The flag-waving to drive multiple new works out of our existing one in short order doesn't account for the elements that result in short-term net losses rather than gains. But it's a reality of any growing market. Proficient investment advisers caution their clients not to watch the daily fluctuations of the Dow Jones Industrial Average. They'll recommend consistent investments in vetted, promising funds, and then let it ride.

The stock market has consistently proven to be the best outlet for return on investment over any ten-year period in American history, but the growth never follows a steady incline. The Dow endures major dips, market corrections, recessions, and other instabilities resulting in short-term, even medium-term losses. On average, the stock market posts a net negative return rate one out of every four years. But the long-term return proves its overall health.

Spiritual transformation—if that's how we want our church to grow—will follow a very similar pattern. And in terms of church expansion and multiplication, we've got to factor in the negative hits we'll invariably take. Sometimes just staying plateaued in a down market is a remarkable sign of health.

2. Spiritual movements don't start because someone decides to start them. My brother Mark, who is one of the most gifted and catalytic guys I know, always theorized anyone could start a fashion trend, especially given the wacko styles introduced during Fashion Week every year. He set out to prove it once, and decided to launch a new fad, hanging shoelaces around his neck as a sort of accent piece to his outfit. He bought sets of different colored laces to match different shirts and styles, and he began boldly wearing them in public. He's one of the gutsiest guys around, and he wore them confidently, waiting for the multitudes to kick in and follow.

They never did. Mostly they just looked at him cockeyed, wondering if he forgot to lace his shoes. We laugh about it now, but he still insists it could catch on someday.

Fashion trends are hard enough, but spiritual movements are another beast altogether.

Here's the thing about spiritual movements: They don't start because someone decides it's time. True spiritual movements are strictly the domain and prerogative of God. He ignites them when *he* decides he wants to, and he doesn't announce in advance when they're coming. Study any of what we'd call major spiritual "revivals" in the world since the completion of Scripture—the Reformation, the Great Awakenings, Azusa Street. Countless studies have been done to identify common themes behind their emergence. You'll read about deep spiritual need, a long-term prayer effort asking God for revival, a group of (usually) younger people at the center of it, and an event that triggered it.

You know what you won't find, in any of them? An individual who intended to start a revival. When the "movement" occurred, it sprang up almost as a side effect. It came out of nowhere. The people at its core had no intention of igniting a movement; they were just living out their faith. God swept in and did something logic-defying. Those who witnessed its inception only recognized it as a revival after the fact.

Even "Shirtless Dancing Guy" didn't start dancing with the purpose of getting the entire crowd to dance. He was just expressing his (more than likely alcohol-aided) freedom. The "movement" broke out spontaneously.

Patrick Morley, author of the classic book *The Man in the Mirror,* compiled ten characteristics of revivals and awakenings through history. Among them were times of moral/spiritual decline, prayer for revival, the preaching of God's word, and the conviction of the Holy Spirit. Honestly, when has there *not* been a time when those factors were all present? Morley wisely went on to reflect that "history tells us that national revivals and awakenings cannot be manufactured. They are sovereign acts of mercy and grace by God himself, when he supernaturally achieves in a short span what seems otherwise impossible."[7]

When we think about our church multiplying itself, absolutely, we train people to step forward to be part of the next kingdom outpost. Without question we invest, envision, and work to enact further expansion from our base. But the creation of a multiplying movement is something we can't manufacture.

3. The Moses delusion. And now we come to the big bubble pop. Studies on biblical leadership don't usually draw much from the Pentateuch. Except, that is, for Moses. We wear out Moses. I've seen and heard more leadership lessons on Moses than any biblical character other than Christ.

The studies generally flow like this:

- Moses was a reluctant leader, but when God called, Moses responded with a faith that trusted in the midst of fear and threat.
- At first, Moses was relegated to sheep-tending in the back forty of the desert, laboring in obscurity, learning faithfulness and humility.
- But when the time came, Moses emerged to lead his people out of slavery through faith-fueled demonstrations of God's power.
- Moses endured intense suffering but paid the price to lead God's nation through the wilderness and bring them to the doorstep of the Promised Land.
- As leaders today, we face the same obstacles as Moses: adversity, lack of self-confidence, and the challenges of impatience and human frailty.
- If we endure like Moses, choose faith, and obey, we can experience the power of God too and accomplish great things in his name.

Moses's story is presented as a vivid, inspiring example for leaders today. God wants to work in similar ways through us, so who will trust him to ignite a movement? Who will step out in faith and in the power of the Most High to see God multiply his impact and blessing? Who will rise up to be the next Moses?

Everybody thinks their story is supposed to parallel Moses's story.

Inspiring as it might be and as well as it preaches, the idea that you're supposed to be Moses is absurd. It's built on *horrible* hermeneutics. Yes, Moses holds the record for mentions in the Hebrews 11 "Faith Hall of Fame." Yes, he stands as one who saw God do miraculous things as a result of trusting him. Absolutely, we can be motivated and encouraged by the fact we serve the same God today. But where does it say *you're* supposed to be this generation's Moses? That you're intended to start a similar movement?

We're guilty of narcissistic exegesis. We insert a subconscious demand that we be the star of the show into our understanding and application of the Scriptures.

Can we please get over ourselves? Show me where it says everybody who plants or pastors a church is supposed to mirror Moses's story. Moses was a one-in-four-hundred-years, hand-selected instrument of God for a very particular time and purpose. God performed once-in-a-millennium miracles to advance his agenda through Moses.

You can be inspired by Moses. You can exhibit faith that mimics Moses's. But you don't get to be Moses.

For every Moses in God's plan, there were a hundred thousand guys named Ralph or George who served God faithfully, sacrificed to obey his ways, led their families well, labored and worshiped and lived and died, without seeing a movement start. Many held leadership positions of one sort or another among God's people. But they were never written about. When their assignments were complete, God welcomed them into his presence with celebration. Their place in the kingdom is revered and secure. But they didn't launch any movements.

You don't choose to be Moses. Heck, *Moses* didn't choose to be Moses. He was dragged kicking and screaming into the role of movement launcher. In truth, if Moses were here to weigh in on the topic, he'd probably insist that God chose to use reluctant, regular, old Moses as a way of proving that *God himself* is the only real movement maker.

You and I are the Ralphs and Georges, the Kevins and Justins—regular guys invited by God to serve as his instruments in the planting of churches that will reach a generation with the gospel. Yes, we sow the seeds of multiplication in our churches from the get-go. Sure, we invest in reproduction. But leave the pressure to start a movement in the hands of the one who's solely responsible for it in the first place.

IF YOU PLANT ONE CHURCH IN A GENERATION, YOU'VE DONE WELL

Please don't gauge a church, or your church, by where it lands on the spectrum of declining-plateaued-growing-birthing-multiplying at any given moment. It might be a thing of wonder that you've just held your own in the face of all the mess you've had to deal with. Such a church should be celebrated, not asked why they're not at a higher level.

I had the privilege of pastoring a church I planted for more than twenty-one years. I've never worked at anything so hard, for so long, in my entire life. Through those years some exceptionally talented people rose up to contribute in ways that humbled and amazed us. The level of excellence we saw emerge from that group was something I'm immensely proud of to this day. There were many times we'd walk away from a Sunday service and say to ourselves, "That may be the best experience any church in the country had today."

But something else was true throughout the duration of my time there. Not once did we ever experience a three-month period during which it felt like we consistently gained momentum, or were even growing. We might have a good week or two, and then we'd see things swing back down. Any time we were asked whether attendance was increasing, we would reflect honestly and say, "Well, we're kind of plateaued right now. Or maybe declining a bit." We were always lean, always struggling, always vulnerable. We regularly repeated what became a pet phrase: "It always feels like a house of cards."

And that's what made the long-term progress almost surreal. Because over that span of years, we did grow. We'd occasionally look back and be reminded how we didn't have this asset or that number of groups or such-and-such level of offering two years earlier. We'd scratch our heads and say, "When did that happen?" We'd reread our audacious strategic plan from a particular year, laugh at how ludicrous it sounded compared to what actually happened, and then realize that eventually much of it did happen . . . far more slowly, in ways we didn't even notice at the time.

Paul was a church planter. He was also an apostle, specially selected by Christ to initiate the spread of the gospel message to new places. But isn't it curious how nowhere in Scripture, when Paul sends his cohorts to help his baby churches develop, does he instruct them to measure themselves by how quickly they become a rapid-multiplication center? Rather, he tells Titus and Timothy to do things like appoint elders, oversee community service, train people in holy living, and take up collections for other bodies in need.

Does that mean those churches weren't supposed to spread out and reach other areas? Of course not. But it at least suggests their assignment wasn't measured first and foremost by the speed and number of daughter churches each planted.

Most of the guys I work with would love for God to choose

them to spawn a movement. They would be thrilled if their church could become a multiplication center out of which dozens of new churches would emerge. To a man, they want the entire world to be reached with the transforming power of the gospel—to a man! They all wave that banner; they all invite their people to make the sacrifices and commitments necessary to become a sending church. They don't lack for zeal, vision, or willingness to sacrifice.

So please don't tell them they just need to dream bigger, or that if they step out in a higher degree of faith God is looking to launch a movement through them. Let's celebrate their faithfulness and resource their efforts, rather than measure them by whether or not they manufactured a revival.

IF GOD MAKES YOU MOSES, BE MOSES

The point is not just that you don't *get* to be Moses; it's that you're not *supposed* to be Moses, either. Aspire to the greatest impact you can make. Serve faithfully. Preach to fifty with the same passion and excellence you would if you were preaching to five thousand. But don't take on the weight of pressure that implies you aren't fully accomplishing your purpose unless you launch a movement that births dozens, if not hundreds, of churches. You don't get to decide that.

If God does choose to make yours an exponentially multiplying church—if you're the next Moses—great! Be Moses with all the fervor and vigor you have. But if you're not, know that it's not because you didn't work hard enough or set your sights high enough.

AND IF YOU'RE RALPH, BE FULLY RALPH

When the late fitness legend Jack LaLanne was in his nineties, he was asked what one piece of advice he would give for staying in shape as a person ages. He gave a very simple answer: "Just keep moving." To those who are planting and leading churches, let's change the narrative for what constitutes fulfilling our calling and vision. You're a raging success if you simply keep moving.

That may mean moving through times of regression and loss. It may mean moving during seasons of plateaued growth. But just keep moving. Keep leading, keep envisioning, keep preaching the truth. When you continue casting vision and empowering people to reach the lost, when you continue investing in and raising up leaders, when you continue loving people and creating an environment that honors God's Word and way . . . you're doing everything God asks of you.

CHAPTER 9

THE TRUTH ABOUT HOW YOU'RE VIEWED

or

Everybody's Kingdom-Minded
Until You Show Up

Some of Hollywood's best acting happens at the annual awards shows.

The Academy Award nominees are announced, and for weeks leading up to the big event you hear all the perfunctory "It's an honor just to be nominated" statements. Then the telecast begins; the category is announced; and they plop a camera directly in front of each nominee's face as their names are read. Side-by-side video footage of all the hopefuls fills a giant screen as the envelope is opened and the winner is announced. Everyone studies the faces—often the losers' even more than the winners'—just to watch their expressions as "the Oscar goes to . . ."

There's the external reaction, required by law to be gracious and professional. The non-winners nod in agreement, clap politely, and smile.

And then there's the internal reaction, which no one ever cops to. Because, unless the acting community consists entirely of nonhumans (a discussion for another day), they're surely feeling something quite different inside than what they express outwardly in that moment. Careers are made on the results of Oscar night. There's no way on earth any warm-blooded mortal isn't desperately hoping his or her name will be the one called.

I understand the attempt at being classy, but just once, I'd like to see a loser react by throwing their hands in the air, rolling their eyes, and slumping backward in genuine disappointment. Such a person would be roasted on social media, but I'd give them big points for transparency.

WHO'S IN THE STANDS?

When a church planter launches a new work, the stands are filled with observers keenly interested in how the adventure will go. The ones who matter most to the planter—beyond his target audience of lost people—offer signs of full, unfettered support. But often they internally view the planter and measure the project's success in ways very different from those they portray externally.

Three entities in particular tend to say one thing but feel another. We do well to be aware of the disparity within each, because on some level their true perspectives will have a bearing on what we can expect from them and how they will affect us.

Hang on, this could be a bumpy ride.

1. Established Churches in the Area

Before we go any further, a caveat: What I'm about to say, I'm not declaring as categorically true. Plenty of like-minded churches offer generous, sincere support to new church plants nearby.

What I am saying, though, is that something is far more common than anyone warns you it will be: established churches in your target planting area aren't nearly as supportive as they claim to be.

They'll welcome you to town. They'll say they're glad you're doing what you're doing. They'll tell you they're available to help in any way they can. But beneath their cordial exterior lies the next dirty little secret of church planting: many feel threatened by a newcomer entering their "territory."

It'll show up through side conversations you'll hear second-hand, a growing standoffishness, and especially the way they respond to tangible opportunities to help.

See, they've worked hard to gain whatever "market share" they hold, and you're the new burger joint opening down the block from theirs. There are only so many beef eaters in town, so any progress you make represents customers who won't be patronizing their place. Almost no one will come out and admit this, even to themselves, but in the darker corners of their minds they see you, on some level, as competition.

So That's What "Territorial" Means

When I first arrived in Columbus, Ohio, to plant, I reached out to anybody I knew in ministry to get the lay of the land and find some camaraderie. I recalled that a fellow student I'd spent some time with in seminary had planted a church nearby about a decade earlier and had seen it grow significantly. So I gave him a call.

It took multiple attempts to elicit any response. Finally, his administrative assistant returned my call and asked if she could help me. When I relayed how I simply wanted to reconnect on a personal level, she reluctantly set up a phone appointment. I finally got through to him, and after he referred me to one of his staff pastors who was "more involved with community outreach," I told him what I'd actually hoped for was just to get coffee together sometime and catch up on how things had gone for him since our seminary days. He let me know he didn't have time for that, but he did say the area was pretty saturated with churches right now, and he honestly didn't think there was much need for a new church plant.

In my mind (and thankfully not out loud), I responded, *Oh, I didn't realize all the lost people around here had been reached.* I decided I probably didn't want that coffee with him after all.

He did eventually offer to spend some time with me, however. A few months later, after my wife had taken our young daughter to participate in their children's program while we were in the early stages of planting, he called to say he and some of his elders wanted to get together with me and some of my elders (of which I, of course, had none) to discuss whether she was bringing our child to their program to recruit their people to our church.

I wished I'd thought of that.

I was appalled, but I shouldn't have been surprised. That mentality may be fleshly, but it's also normative and long-standing. As early as the first century, the competitive spirit undermined the work of the gospel. All the "I follow Paul," "I follow Apollos," "I follow Cephas" nonsense in Corinth (1 Corinthians 1:12) sprang from the same seedbed. It's human nature to look at others trying to do the same thing we're trying to do and compare ourselves to them.

Ironically, the bigger and more secure the church, the more protective of their turf they can become. Church planters in the same town tend to support each other freely. And why not? They're foxhole buddies, keenly aware they're fighting the same foe and glad to cling to one another. But established churches can become self-protective and paranoid. They may speak kindly on the surface, but don't be surprised if they don't bend over backward to offer you tangible help.

During our first church plant endeavor near Los Angeles, we lived across the street from the largest church in town. I'd met the senior pastor, who was initially very cordial and affirming. So we got the bright idea that perhaps our core group's kids could take part in their midweek program while we held core meetings in our home. I asked, and the pastor's tone changed noticeably. He responded that they'd be "uncomfortable" with that—not because the parents wouldn't technically be on the premises, or even because we weren't members of the church, but because, and I quote, "Let's be honest, we're kind of in competition."

Yes, we were quite the threat. They had twelve hundred members; we had five families.

Shortly after we began our Ohio plant, an established pastor in a nearby suburb invited me to lunch, and we had a nice, amiable conversation. He ended it by saying, "I'm glad you're here. If there's anything we can do to help, just let us know."

Now, as an aside, when people say that last phrase, they're usually being polite. They don't actually expect you to come up with something that would cost them anything to help. It's like asking, "How are you?" The only appropriate answer is, "Fine."

But not knowing any better than to believe he meant it, sometime later I contacted him again. "I was thinking about your offer," I said, "and there might actually be a way you could be of help to us."

"Oh . . . really?" he replied. "What is it?"

"If you could mention us to your folks, maybe let them know we're getting started, and if they've got unchurched friends or relatives in our area who are open to hearing about a church starting close to them and could recommend us to them, we'd love to get those contacts and meet them."

Long pause.

"I'm afraid I can't do that," he said.

Caught by surprise, I inquired, "Oh . . . can I ask why not?"

"Because of the theological differences," he replied.

We hadn't talked about our theology when we'd met. So I told him I was a bit confused about how he could know of any differences. He responded, "Well, because if there weren't any, you'd be in our denomination."

I didn't even know what to do with that.

Sadly, the admonition in 1 John 3:18 to not love just with words, but with actions and in truth, is lost on a lot of established church pastors when they interact with church planters. They can be really adroit at verbalizing their support, but behind the veil, many view you as more rival than teammate.

Veteran quarterbacks are generally perturbed when their team drafts a young quarterback, even if they say publicly they're looking forward to mentoring him. Don't take it personally if at some point you discover your effort is being criticized or looked at suspiciously by area pastors who had initially reacted positively when you arrived, or whom you might not have even met. They may not be consciously aware they're reacting out of their insecurities.

It's Easier to Shoot a Stranger Than a Friend

Allow me to suggest one way to combat the fears that may arise among nearby established churches. Rather than write these churches off when they keep you at arm's length, or react with resentment when you hear you've been devalued by another ministry in town, go out of your way to initiate direct contact with them. Keep asking until you can get an audience with their lead pastor, and then let him know you're glad to be joining him in the battle; tell him you respect and are grateful for his church's presence in the community.

Then talk about the elephant in the room, and give him your word you will never target anyone who is already part of another church. Assure him you want to grow solely by reaching unchurched people with the gospel. Grant him overt permission to call you should he ever hear of anyone from his place defecting to yours (and some may). Then keep in regular contact, reiterating your message and affirming him for his church's important influence in the community. It's a preemptive strike to thwart the enemy's subversive attempts to divide you. But it also may open the door to authentic cooperation and dialogue in the future.

Genuine kingdom-minded churches do exist. During a pivotal season for our young church, we were completely striking out as we tried to find a place to hold an important vision event. Another church in town heard about our plight. What they did next astounded us. They not only invited us to use their building free of charge; they committed to allowing us access for as many future gatherings as we might need. They had no stake in our project and had nothing to gain. They simply said they remembered what it was like.

I could have kissed them.

At that moment I vowed to do the same for future new churches in our area should we ever have the chance. Several years later, we were able to open our own doors to more than one plant that needed a place to meet.

If you lead a church that substantively blesses new churches around you, thank you! If you can become one, know that the fragrance of the gospel wafts over the entire community every time you extend that rare brand of grace.

2. Denominational Headquarters and Sponsor Churches/Organizations

Once again, let me cover my tracks by stating that there are outstanding exceptions to this. But here's another reality of the church planting realm: When someone invests in something, they expect results. And when it comes to new churches, these results—regardless of how much talk there may be about faithfulness and heart transformation—almost always come down to the big three B's: Bodies, Budgets, and Buildings.

When folks from a supporting church or denomination ask a church planter how the work is going, the first question is typically something like, "How many are you running these days?" "What's the size of the church?" "What's your average Sunday attendance?" Focus all you want on the inroads you're making, the relationships you're building, the people you're serving. All they hear are the hard numbers.

I consulted with a gifted church planter whose mother church sent them out with fifty adults and high hopes because their previous planting project had grown to multiple hundreds in a couple years using an identical method with roughly the same sized launch team. His group birthed with great fanfare and worked their tails off, and after eighteen months they had about seventy-five adults regularly involved.

The sponsor church shut them down.

They decided the effort "just wasn't working" and called everyone back to the mother ship. The planter was informed they couldn't defend supporting the church any further when it wasn't moving forward at a rate that justified the investment.

They'd seen attendance increase by 50 percent in a year and a half. They'd witnessed salvation decisions and multiple baptisms. They were well on their way to becoming self-supporting. Their church was already equal to the median-sized church in America! And they were dubbed a failure.

In the business world, as a rule of thumb, the average small business requires three years before it will turn any profit whatsoever, and five years before it can be considered established. Malcolm Gladwell concluded in his book *Outliers* that mastering any skill requires ten thousand hours of practice—which equates to forty hours per week, fifty weeks per year, for five years.[1] Most church planters aren't afforded half that to prove they've got the chops—or the tangible results—to be deemed a success.

Those supporting you financially have timelines and conditions for how long they'll keep it up. Success equals self-supporting status, and if you're not making progress toward it relatively quickly, they may pat you on the head and say, "Good boy," but they're worried.

When denominations decide to release valuable assets to a particular person and project, there are most certainly strings attached. Some expectations are made overtly clear—faithfulness, loyalty, work ethic, responsibility. But it's the unstated ones that are often more concrete. They want to hear success stories. They want to see numbers. They want to be paid back, in one form or another.

Sending agencies and denominations hold the power of blessing and cursing in their hands simply by how they navigate church planter financial support decisions. Those who bring the funding hammer down swiftly and decisively in the name of fiscal prudence can crush a planter's spirit—not to mention their livelihood—in a single blow. Those who balance financial accountability with relational value, respect, and (above all) patience can breathe life and grace into a planter, even when the news they ultimately have to deliver is less than positive.

Then there's the whole, "Are you in your own building yet?" thing. If you continue to meet in rented facilities long term, there are those who won't consider you legitimately established until you've put up brick and mortar. They keep waiting for the day you'll break ground on your own building and realize the dream of becoming a "real church." That phrase will infuriate you. But easy there, Geppetto; they can't help themselves. It's all many of them have ever known.

You can teach that the church isn't a building till your lips fall off, but you're always going to fly against the headwind of those who gauge your success by how quickly you can hang out a shingle on your own digs.

You certainly don't need more pressure about any of this, but you do need to be aware that when it comes to sponsoring groups and churches, there's almost always an invisible clock ticking. The more cognizant you are of that, the more steps you can take to mitigate its pressure.

One of those steps may be giving strong consideration to planting bivocationally. The trend toward bivocational planters is actually a healthy one, because it relieves both you and your sponsoring group of the awkward decision to cut support when it means leaving a bunch of hungry mouths unfed.

The North American Mission Board, the Southern Baptist Convention's domestic church planting wing, lists three benefits of bivocational church planting:

- missional engagement
- financial stability
- shared leadership[2]

Bivocational work affords you a built-in mission field and opens natural doors for personal outreach. It also keeps your perspective fresh on how unchurched people think and live. Yes, being bivocational decreases your available hours and diverts some of your attention. It can certainly slow the progress. But read chapter 7 again. You could work a hundred hours a week, and it more than likely wouldn't increase your growth rate or hasten your pace much anyway. Bivo isn't a bad idea. Consider it.

Even if you're "lucky" and have a couple of deep-pocket supporters, do the extra work to diversify and spread your support base. Otherwise, if you lose one or two of those you're most dependent on—including the sponsor church's budget or denominational coffers—you're up a creek. Don't think they won't do it. They've got a date and a number in mind, even if they aren't saying it. You may not know you've reached it until the email comes informing you they're "reevaluating" their involvement.

3. Your Own Internal Gauge

A little-known '70s slasher movie titled *Black Christmas* coined a chilling phrase, later made famous by *When a Stranger Calls*: "The calls are coming from *inside the house*."[3]

Your worst enemy when it comes to jaded perceptions and hidden expectations might actually be living under your own roof. Your most dubious evaluator may very well be calling from inside your own head.

If you're sure this part doesn't apply to you, feel free to skip to the next chapter. But it might be worth your while to hang with me here, because chances are you're carrying a self-imposed standard of productivity and performance so deeply rooted in your soul that it dictates your mood most waking hours. Even if no one else is demanding that you display a particular rate of progress, you demand it of yourself.

It can trace back to any number of sources—a compulsion to live up to the investment others have made in you, the need to earn your earthly father's approval, an internal demand to prove your own worth. You've had prophetic utterances pronounced over you. Elderly saints have declared, "You're going to do great things for God." When they commissioned you to plant a daughter church, sincere supporters pulled you aside and whispered in your ear, "You know, I don't think it's going to be very long before the baby outgrows the mother."

But most of all, it's likely you carry a stubborn attachment between your job performance and your standing with the Father in heaven. It fuels a relentless compulsion to measure up, to exceed expectations, to continually prove your worth to yourself and to God.

If you don't break free from that compulsion, you'll continue to be dogged by the need to produce, produce, produce. And when those you're leading don't respond to your prompts, you'll start beating the sheep instead of shepherding them.

INITIATING COUNTERMEASURES

The bondage of compulsion isn't broken by preaching on it or by merely confessing it. It can only be dislodged through sustained exposure of your soul to God's unfiltered, extravagant grace. And that's why it is critically important that you find ways to regularly plunge yourself beneath its waterfall.

Sometimes the most productive thing a church planter can do is get away for protracted periods of time with his Bible and some Henri Nouwen books. Initiate a silent retreat where you focus singularly on the supreme worth that God freely dispenses on you without condition. Read Dallas Willard and Richard Rohr. Breathe in the unfathomable love and worth with which God envelops you here and now, as we speak.

Please don't let it become only an occasional practice for you to retreat for uninterrupted days of re-exposure to God's unqualified value of you, just as you are. Find a spiritual director who will consistently draw you toward full awareness of your irrevocable, most highly favored status with the Savior.

If right about now you find yourself clucking your tongue over how I've gone all touchy-feely on you, you're probably among those who most need what we're talking about. This isn't something you can just check off your to-do list before moving on to more important matters. It's at the very core of your spiritual wholeness.

And it only comes through slow, deep reflection and intense, introspective surrender.

Those of us prone to obsessive productivity need to inhale Romans 4:5, not just exegete it. We need to embrace from our core the truth of Ephesians 3:17–19 (NLT):

> Then Christ will make his home in your hearts as you trust in him. Your roots will grow down into God's love and keep you strong. And may you have the power to understand, as all God's people should, how wide, how long, how high, and how deep his love is. May you experience the love of Christ, though it is too great to understand fully. Then you will be made complete with all the fullness of life and power that comes from God.

Listen to the autobiographical words of Brennan Manning in *The Furious Longing of God*: "The God I've come to know by sheer grace, the Jesus I met in the grounds of my own self, has furiously loved me regardless of my state—grace or disgrace. And why? For His love is never, never, never based on our performance, never conditioned by our moods—of elation or depression. The furious love of God knows no shadow of alteration or change. It is reliable. And always tender."[4]

And a bit more Manning, from *Abba's Child*:

> Years ago, I related a story about a priest from Detroit named Edward Farrell who went on his two-week summer vacation to Ireland. His one living uncle was about to celebrate his eightieth birthday. On the great day, the priest and his uncle got up before dawn and dressed in silence. They took a walk along the shores of Lake Killarney and stopped to watch the sunrise. Standing side by side with not a word

exchanged and staring straight at the rising sun. Suddenly the uncle turned and went skipping down the road. He was radiant, beaming, smiling from ear to ear.

His nephew said, "Uncle Seamus, you really look happy."

"I am, lad."

"Want to tell me why?"

His eighty-year-old uncle replied, "Yes, you see, me Abba is very fond of me."

How would you respond if I asked you this question: "Do you honestly believe God *likes* you, not just loves you because theologically God *has* to love you?" If you could answer with gut-level honesty, "Oh, yes, my Abba is very fond of me," you would experience a serene compassion for yourself that approximates the meaning of tenderness.[5]

It can also free you from your own prison.

NO BIRD FLIES SO FREE AS THE ONE ONCE CAGED

You know this. You've taught it. But hear it again. Pause a moment and open not just your ears but the depth of your heart to absorb it once more.

God has never, ever, once in your life measured you on a scale of timetables or achievement. He embraces you as tightly when you're lazy or stumbling morally as he does when you're lighting up the scoreboard. He provides everything you need, sings over you, and celebrates your very existence, every bit as much when everything is falling backward as when it's surging forward. Right now, at this very moment, even if you never lift another finger to accomplish anything for him, he's fiercely proud of you.

I hope you comprehend that. But let yourself feel it too. Hear him say it directly to you. Allow it to drench you from head to toe and penetrate to your bones, so that it frees you to unclench your gut and loosens the frenzied compulsion to make progress at all costs. Relax, really relax, in a sovereign surety you can never lose.

Then when you get back to the grind, hold on to that perspective when you encounter others who view you as the competition, when friendly fire wings you for not meeting someone's production schedule. You may never match the unspoken expectations of your sending group. Or your parents. Or yourself. But your Father in heaven—the one who will ultimately make sure the bills get paid—isn't holding any clipboards or withholding any favor.

As compulsion's grip is loosened, you'll find yourself more able to do some things that not only exhibit genuine freedom but disarm the effect of others' judgments. You'll be able to laugh at yourself—and your "we didn't come anywhere near meeting that goal" moments—more easily. You'll be able to admit your failures and weaknesses before others even bring them up. You'll be more capable of actually slowing down a little and relishing the journey, even when the journey isn't going anything like you imagined.

No one else in the world uses the scale your true Father uses to gauge your success. And if you can really believe it, no one else's scale matters.

CHAPTER 10

THE TRUTH ABOUT "EXCELLENCE"

or

If You Try to Do Everything Well,
You'll Do Nothing Well

Disney rules the world.

If you've ever taken your children to a Disney theme park—and of course you *must* or risk a visit from Child Protective Services—you know that every square inch and every moment of the experience are meticulously orchestrated. Disney World in Orlando, Florida, fastidiously trains more than 65,000 "cast members" to never miss a detail.

An underground city of tunnels ensures no character is ever seen outside its natural habitat. Staffers smile and enthusiastically address any concern a guest raises. Walt Disney famously required trash receptacles be placed within thirty paces of any point in the park, based on the amount of time he calculated someone will hold a wrapper before dropping it. And you never see workers emptying those waste containers. The same tunnels house a vacuum system jetting trash away at more than sixty miles per hour.[1]

Disney Parks sweat every detail—everything you see, hear, smell, taste, and feel—to maintain the value of absolute excellence. Lee Cockerell, former executive vice president of operations for the Disney World Resort, said, "At Disney, we believe everything's important. Every detail. We don't want any paper on the ground. We're fanatical about [it]—you don't have to be happy to work at Disney, but you do have to act happy for eight hours. Because we're putting on a show."[2]

BOOMERS, MEGACHURCHES, AND "THE PURSUIT"

The same Baby Boomer generation reared on Disney's manufactured utopia gave rise to a new standard for what the local church could and should be. Three contemporary cultural phenomena came to prominence during that era and profoundly affected the evangelical community.

1. **The birth of generational baselining.** Beginning with the close of World War II and continuing to the present day, America's unparalleled run of prolonged economic prosperity spawned what could be called "generational baselining." What one generation labors and sacrifices to achieve, the next assumes as a given—the starting point from which it expects to acquire more.

House sizes serve as a vivid example: Children growing up in a home their parents worked their entire lives to attain presumed that size to be the minimum for their own homeowner expectations. As a result, the average square footage of single-family homes built in the United States increased at an astounding rate during the decades following World War II:

- 1945: 797 square feet
- 1955: 1,170 square feet

- 1965: 1,525 square feet
- 1975: 1,645 square feet
- 1985: 1,785 square feet
- 1995: 2,095 square feet
- 2005: 2,434 square feet
- 2015: 2,740 square feet[3]

As prosperity in the United States continued, generational baselining expanded across multiple platforms of American society—everything from starting salaries and vacation time to luxury item accumulation and customer service expectations. The spectrum extended to include the amenities, facilities, and services provided by the local church.

2. The rise of the megachurch. Skye Jethani likens the proliferation of the megachurch to that of the cruise ship industry. As transatlantic travel shifted from ship to air, astute members of the maritime trade reinvented themselves to offer sea travel as a destination rather than a mode of transportation. Jethani observes, "Similarly, in the mid 20th century the utilitarian role of the church, transporting people into communion with God, was disrupted by secularism. This led innovative pastors to transform churches into destinations rather than vehicles, and attracting irreligious consumers required much larger churches with previously unimaginable offerings. The megachurch explosion began."[4]

The megachurch era ushered in "church as destination"—the concept that one local church could be capable of covering the entire spectrum of human need and spiritual development under one roof. The church became one-stop shopping. There you could find multitiered discipleship tracks, music training, aerobics classes, small groups, Bible studies, men's and women's gatherings, age-specific programs, recovery centers, and ministries targeting practically every need in the community. Jethani describes some of the "unimaginable" services: "Coffee shops, bookstores, health clubs, recreation centers, even auto mechanics and production studios. Just as modern cruise ships have redefined the passenger shipping, today's megachurches have redefined our understanding of ministry."[5]

3. **The elevation of "excellence."** Terry Orlick's *In Pursuit of Excellence* took the American business world by storm in 1980, championing the principle of maximized performance in every aspect of an organization's undertakings.[6] The church, recognizing a natural parallel to God's flawless nature, quickly embraced the ideology and raised a clarion call: a perfect God deserves nothing less than the highest level of excellence that humans can produce in any endeavor representing him.

Some long-overdue modernization resulted. Churches began improving and updating their language, decor, designs, and overall programming quality. "Excellence" became the industry standard for church-produced ministry.

PRESENTING THE "FULL-SERVICE" CHURCH

By the turn of the millennium, these collective influences had essentially reshaped the definition of a "fully functioning" church. A new phrase was born—churches were mandated to be "full-service," offering a comprehensive smorgasbord of thoroughly developed programs delivered with consistently high levels of excellence.

The requirements naturally extended to church plant projects. From their inception, new churches were now expected to provide a full complement of the highest-quality products, including outstanding worship and teaching, exceptional children's areas, trained greeters, comprehensive first steps and discipleship courses, effective missional outreach . . . and coffee—above all, coffee.

PERPETUAL BOLT TIGHTENING

I had just finished pushing our daughter on the backyard swing when the bracket connecting the chains to the crossbar suddenly crashed down, narrowly missing her head. Ready to sue the swing set company for negligence, I pulled out the owner's manual in search of a customer service number and instead noticed the safety instructions. In big, bold letters it recommended tightening all the swing set bolts on a monthly basis.

A monthly basis? I did some quick mental calculations and determined the last time I had tightened those bolts was exactly . . . never. In twelve years. Worse, the fact that I should ensure my children's safety by occasionally tightening swing set bolts had never once crossed my mind, which instantly landed my name on the list of finalists for Worst. Father. Ever.

That got me thinking, so I pulled out all the owners manuals we'd stuffed in a drawer to see what other home maintenance routines I was supposed to be performing. I started a list of all the household items the manufacturers indicated should be inspected, tested, tightened, cleaned, repaired, or replaced at least monthly:

- faucet aerators
- shower heads
- refrigerator drain pan
- dishwasher seals
- kitchen exhaust fan
- heating/cooling air filter
- unused drains
- heat vents and registers
- refrigerator coils
- GFI circuit interrupters

- smoke detectors
- carbon monoxide detectors
- in-sink garbage disposal
- water filter
- soft water appliances
- humidifier plates and drums
- door and window screens
- dryer lint trap
- water heater TPR valve
- bedframes
- chair hardware
- wall anchors
- TV mounts
- plumbing fixtures
- gas appliance connections
- garage door opener
- shelving hardware
- gutters
- downspouts
- roof shingles
- mower blades
- . . . swing set hardware

I had no idea what half that stuff was. I was exhausted just reading it. The list didn't yet include all the annual and semiannual tasks. And I hadn't even gotten to the car.

I put the manuals away, retreated to the couch, and watched some golf.

The "manuals" for church planting these days likewise contain a list of mandatory services expected to be fully operational and finely tuned from Day One:

- worship
- Bible teaching
- prayer
- outreach
- discipleship
- welcome/hospitality
- assimilation
- small groups
- children's ministry
- setup/teardown
- A/V
- leadership development
- men's ministry
- women's ministry
- youth ministry
- counseling
- ministry to the homeless/poor
- addiction recovery
- social media
- special activities (VBS, Christmas events)
- missions involvement

These stand in addition to the myriad of essential support ministries and compulsory organizational requirements, like financial recordkeeping, governmental documentation, background checks, safety protocol, medical emergency provisions . . . ad infinitum.

Contemporary church culture has been conditioned to require the full gamut of services, delivered with excellence, from the outset of any new church.[7] We're told it's what God deserves and our target audience expects.

I'm here to tell you it'll reduce you to lying in a corner, curled up in the fetal position.

DYING IN THE BEST SHAPE OF OUR LIVES

The mandate to do everything at once and do it all well, while largely unchallenged in today's church planting world, is built on an unhealthy—and unattainable—foundation. You may be supremely gifted and extraordinarily driven, but a handful of factors ensure your inability to produce that outcome.

First, you are one person, bound by the limitations of time, energy, and skill. No mere mortal possesses sufficient bandwidth to conceive, design, implement, and exert quality control over everything the full-service model makes you responsible to churn out. You don't own a cape, and if you do, we probably need to have a separate conversation.

Second, your core team is small and, while undoubtedly sincere, full of people who are, as Larry Osborne observed, only willing to give two time slots per week to the cause.[8] What took megachurches years of funding, development, and an army of volunteers to produce is physically impossible for a typical church planting core group to replicate, even if we assume (and we shouldn't) it's an accurate picture of what a fully functioning church should be.

And third, it's not the falling swing that will kill you; it's all the bolt tightening. Even if you somehow sacrifice and overwork to the point where you erect a basic framework for full-spectrum ministry, the inevitable problem solving and maintenance will leave you running haplessly from one front to another, until you and your team collapse from exhaustion under a barrage of falling chains.

If you try to do everything well, you'll do nothing well.

REPLACING "BALANCE" WITH "RHYTHM"

I want to suggest a contrarian alternative to the full-service, everything-with-excellence picture of church. And it starts with replacing what I'll call the myth of "balance" with the health of "rhythm."

"Balance" is a concept suggesting that every important element of a life or organization can be given consistent, equitable time and energy. Christian circles have long embraced the goal of a maintained, equalized lifestyle that produces stability and wholeness—the balanced Christian life.

The balanced life is a lovely notion, but it's a unicorn. No one has ever seen one, because it doesn't exist. If "balance" means keeping all of life's priorities at a consistently equal level for an extended period of time, no one in history has ever lived a balanced life—including the Buddhists, from whom modern pop Christianity may have borrowed the idea in the first place.

I'm aware that a myriad of good and even vital involvements *should* consistently be built into my schedule. I *should* exercise my body, pray and read Scripture, spend quality time with my wife and children, work to provide for my family, build relationships with unbelievers, serve those I see in need, sleep eight hours a night, maintain my home, check on my elderly neighbors, etc., etc. In theory, every one of those is important—even "essential"— enough to warrant attention every day of my life.

But maintaining them all in consistent balance is an impossible task. Life throws surprises at us. Crises arise. Opportunities knock. Deadlines crunch. Interruptions interrupt. I can confidently say I've never experienced a single day where I could report, "Today I kept everything in balance."

By contrast, a life "rhythm" means addressing important elements progressively and intentionally, majoring on one to the temporary exclusion of others, with a view to eventually addressing all. But this rhythm never places us under any compulsion to squeeze them all into one day, or even one season.

Ecclesiastes 3 expresses this beautifully. Everything under

heaven—all the chief activities of life—have distinct seasons when they become the focus. There's a time to cry, and a time to laugh; a time to work, and a time to rest; a time to gather stones, and a time to scatter them (Ecclesiastes 3:1–8). They're not simultaneously balanced. They're each done in their appropriate season, in an intentional rhythm.

Apply that to a local church's ministry. No church has ever been capable of maintaining the highest possible excellence and priority for every ministry simultaneously. We can't keep all the bolts tightened all the time. Rather, we address the ones we deem most important in a particular season, knowing that in time we'll give attention to them all.

JESUS THE IMBALANCED

Allow me to play the Jesus card here. It could be argued that at any given moment, Jesus' ministry was anything but "balanced."

The gospels depict long stretches where Jesus concentrates on one activity and appears to neglect others. For days on end, we see him preaching and healing, ostensibly disregarding the practice of personal rest and Sabbath (for which he was roundly attacked). Scripture records him working on the Sabbath more than it does resting on it.

For other extended periods, it seems all Jesus does is pray. He's escaping from the throngs, going off by himself, "as was his custom" (Luke 22:39 ESV). He's praying all night; he's praying all day. During those seasons, there's no mention of his spending time with lost people, caring for the poor, or investing in his disciples.

On still other occasions, Jesus appears to have forgotten all about spiritual formation. He preaches the gospel and then immediately moves on to other towns, presumably ignoring follow-up and discipleship.

Jesus didn't seem particularly interested in "balancing" his ministry, and he never instructed his followers to give equal attention to every component of God's purposes simultaneously. What he did do was maintain a healthy rhythm, a string of systematic imbalances that, when observed over extended time, addressed everything he deemed important.

The thirty-thousand-foot view reveals how Jesus covered the entire spectrum of ministry—everything from prayer, evangelism, and discipleship to worship, human need, and personal rest. He completed entirely the work the Father had given him to do (John 17:4). He simply did so at an unfrenzied pace, under no compulsion to keep them balanced in a given season. He modeled the same lifestyle he offered his followers—"the unforced *rhythms* of grace" (Matthew 11:28 MSG, italics added).

ENACTING A LEADERSHIP RHYTHM

If we resist the gravitational pull to provide every service imaginable, all at once from the outset, we can establish a healthy rhythm that keeps us sane while fulfilling the church's mission. Allow me to suggest a handful of practices to enact such a rhythm:

1. **Do one or two things well.** Gary Keller, cofounder of Keller Williams Realty, underscored the principle of isolating *the* singular most important thing an organization exists to do, and the importance of concentrating its energies on it. His book, *The One Thing*, offered these assertions:

- It is not that we have too little time to do all the things we need to do; it is that we feel the need to do too many things in the time we have.[9]
- The more things you do, the less successful you are at any one of them.[10]

- You need to be doing fewer things for more effect instead of doing more things with side effects.[11]
- Success is built sequentially. It's one thing at a time.[12]

Paul's words in Philippians 3:13 (NLT)—"I focus on this one thing"—may not have been written as a prescription for church planting, but the principle behind them can certainly be applied to how we establish a church's identity. Ask yourself what you and your church's core are capable of doing best right now, without having to hire anyone new or force yourselves to produce something for which you're not equipped. Let that become the anchor point for your early ministry.

If you've got the resources to produce outstanding music and worship, make that your calling card. If your core includes a disproportionate number of gifted schoolteachers and passionate children's workers, give them a wide berth to place children's ministry front and center.

If your preaching and teaching is the best thing you've got going for you (and you may want to ask several others before assuming that's the case), feature it as the main draw. If there's a deep trove of praying people committed to interceding for and with each other, make prayer groups your centerpiece. If your core people are exceptionally good at creating heart-level, transformative community in groups, lead with that.

This doesn't mean other "essentials" of church ministry aren't important. You simply play to your strengths, and allow time for other, equally important aspects of spiritual community to develop.

2. Provide basic, minimum coverage of the rest. SafeAuto Insurance carved out a market niche by specializing in bare-bones auto insurance for those with limited income. Their policies offered just enough to meet the minimum coverage required by law. Their tagline was, "We keep you legal for less." They recognized that was all many customers could afford. It may not be ideal, but at least it covers the bases.

Whatever church model you're following, you have a set of absolute necessities you know must be in place by your launch date. I'm not here to argue for a particular list, but I am urging you to conscientiously think it through and decide what you simply cannot start without. Then take that list and find a way to offer, like the auto insurer, "minimum coverage" for most, while you invest in the one or two you consider to be of utmost importance.

Can that approach be biblical? Think of the apostles in Acts 6. Human need and care for the poor and widowed was overwhelming them. They had the audacity to prioritize their available hours and determine they needed to be freed from that responsibility in order to dedicate their energies to "prayer and the ministry of the word" (verse 4).

At that moment they could have been accused of devaluing a key function of the church, of considering administering a food program (verse 2) beneath them. But they granted themselves permission to not give everything the same level of personal attention. So they instructed those they were shepherding to "choose seven men" and "turn this responsibility over to them" (verse 3). They directed their attention to one or two things and made provision enough for the other things to ensure they would be covered.

I call this "the art of strategic neglect." Determine the areas you're simply not going to consider a priority for a season. Allow them to function in maintenance mode, knowing you have a plan to heighten their quality at a later date. As author-composer Robert Fritz wrote, "If something is worth doing, it's worth doing poorly until you can do it well."[13]

Then focus on your chosen priority, make it top-shelf, and live with the tension of not doing everything else equally well.

You'll say "no" a lot and "not now" even more. But you'll free yourself from the compulsion to perform the impossible.

3. Own the criticism. Not buying into the demand to be a full-service church will unquestionably lead to criticism and complaint, and nobody likes to be criticized.

In our church plant's early attempts to avoid disappointing anyone, we wound up disappointing everyone. So we made a conscious decision: We'd be the first to admit we weren't going to improve particular areas, or even provide some at all. We openly declared our willingness to allow some of our requisite programs to limp along for a while. While we had a plan to make them better someday, we were more committed to health than to impressions, so we chose to accept the criticisms and affirm their accuracy. It was amazing how well that disarmed people's complaints.

Be the first to admit you're not offering everything a church can offer. Be up front about the intentionality behind it. Assure the critics you're aware of it, and that there's a plan to improve the area they're faulting one day. But make it clear that day is not today. If they believe you should move it up the priority list, tell them you'll be happy to pass their thoughts along to your decision-making team, who always appreciates input.

You may never be hired to run Disney World, but you'll avoid winding up in the fetal position.

4. Tap into what others are already offering elsewhere. A group of neighbors living in a cul-de-sac made a brilliant discovery: Occasionally, they all would need various tools they didn't possess—a heavy-duty snowblower after major winter storms, an extension ladder to clean their gutters, an air compressor when a tire went flat. Rather than go out and make major purchases for the same stuff they couldn't fit in their garages anyway, they each bought one of the items and shared them with one another on the rare occasions they needed one.

The pressure to create your own program for every ministry under the sun is sometimes rooted in an ugly hubris. We feel the need for everything in which our people participate to bear our tattoo. But as the expression says, "It's amazing how much can get done when it doesn't matter who gets the credit." Does another church in your area offer a program your people could benefit from—a support group, a recovery program, a school, a Bible Study Fellowship class? Ask if you can send folks their way. Encourage your attendees to take advantage of what the larger body of Christ is doing. Don't reinvent the wheel.

About a year into our Ohio church plant, a group of parents approached me and insisted we start our own Vacation Bible School. But two other churches in town were well-known for investing more than $50,000 each in their VBS weeks every summer. They printed custom T-shirts, constructed elaborate props like full-scale pirate ships and realistic moonscapes, and brought in special guests. Their VBS programs were spectacular. Why drain our already-too-busy people to replicate (with surely inferior results) something already existing down the block, just so we could control what happens or put our name on it? So we told them, "There's already somebody doing this better than we ever could. Go be part of it. Offer to volunteer if they need help. Give some money there if you can to contribute to their costs." They did just that; everyone went home happy; and I got a free T-shirt out of the deal.

Let someone else be the "cool VBS church" in town. You'll live.

5. Target one area per year for improvement. This is where you stir intentionality into your rhythm. If you start with your eggs in just one or two baskets, you can introduce additional baskets one at a time without breaking the eggs. Prayerfully discern one area per year whose development you sense would most benefit your body. Cast a vision for participation in it. Then design and execute it well.

Establishing a rhythm of a one-per-year emphasis enables you to maintain quality in your existing ministries while expanding needed areas at a healthy pace. It also allows for newer attendees to step up and step in to help develop these new areas.

Even so, remember to grant your longtimers permission to shift their level of involvement in the areas into which they've previously immersed themselves. You can't expect everyone to simply conjure up extra margin to accommodate the additions without clearing some space.

When you do that, you're leading with a whole lot of rhythm. And a reduced amount of blues.

A RISING TIDE

We aren't often afforded the luxury of a thirty-thousand-foot view of where we've been and where we're going. But when it comes to expectations for programs and the excellence with which they're done, the wide view is always the most important one. At any given moment, the list of things we wish we were doing better will be long and aggravating. If you're a strong leader, you'll always carry that mental list around with you.

But if you can maintain a healthy rhythm while resisting the pressure to spin every plate to its highest possible speed, something will happen over time: You'll notice how the rising tide has slowly lifted all the boats. Your people will have grown substantively; your ministries will have achieved consistent levels of quality; and you'll see maturing believers seek out involvements far more because of what it produces in their hearts than because of how good it makes your church look.

CHAPTER 11

THE TRUTH ABOUT LEADERSHIP

or

Colonel Jessup Was Right

Top 10 lists of "Greatest Leaders in History" consistently include some familiar names:

- Alexander the Great
- Julius Caesar
- Attila the Hun
- William Wallace
- Joan of Arc
- Napoleon Bonaparte
- Abraham Lincoln
- Martin Luther King Jr.
- . . . and, quite often, Jesus of Nazareth.

These figures share some characteristics commonly associated with strong leadership: a deeply held cause, profound courage, the ability to motivate and mobilize great numbers of followers, tenacity . . . and one more—an early death.

Leaders, it seems, pay a price.

SO FEW LEADERS,
FOR SUCH GOOD REASONS

For pastoral leaders, the price tag can even include additional surcharges. A local church pastor endures all the universal challenges of leadership—risk aversion, change resistance, heightened criticism. But they also face the added hurdles of leading a chronically underfunded, not-for-profit, predominantly volunteer organization toward a largely thankless task, all while being directly opposed by supernaturally powered evil.

Peter Drucker, the late leadership guru, was widely quoted as saying the nation's four most difficult leadership positions are (1) president of the United States, (2) president of a university, (3) CEO of a hospital, and (4) pastor of a church—and not necessarily in that order.[1] Anyone who has served as a pastor for any length of time nods in painful agreement.

The statistics back it up:

- 84 percent of pastors say they're on call twenty-four hours a day.
- 80 percent expect conflict in their church.
- 54 percent find the role of pastor frequently overwhelming.
- 48 percent often feel the demands of ministry are more than they can bear.[2]
- Only one in twenty who enter pastoral ministry will retire from it.[3]

Pastoral leaders suffer. Deeply. Undeservedly. Disproportionately.

It's no wonder the church runs at a perpetual leadership deficit. Aspiring to lead is like leaning into a right hook. Factor in the additional demands of entrepreneurship required to church plant, and we shouldn't be surprised that most potential recruits run screaming from the building.

But for all the documented costs attached to leading a church planting effort, the highest toll is exacted by factors that are seldom mentioned or even recognized. We learn to anticipate the big blows associated with leading, but no one warns us about the cumulative effect of the smaller ones.

IT'S NOT THE CONCUSSIONS, IT'S THE REPEATED HITS

Few had ever heard of Chronic Traumatic Encephalopathy, or CTE, before the early 2000s, when studies linked the degenerative brain disease to former National Football League players exhibiting behavioral and mood problems, violent and suicidal tendencies, and early dementia. Once the connection was made public, many major contact sports leagues began instituting concussion protocols. Players observed to be woozy after a severe blow to the head were immediately removed from the game and checked for signs of concussion in an attempt to ward off the brain trauma responsible for CTE.

But further study revealed a surprising twist. Boston University researchers released findings showing CTE doesn't result primarily from the effects of severe concussions. Rather, it stems from the cumulative effect of repeated hits to the head, regardless of their severity.[4] Dr. Lee Goldstein, coauthor of the study, told the *Washington Post*, "The concussion is really irrelevant for triggering CTE . . . It's really the hit that counts."[5]

The cost of leadership for a church planter follows a similar pattern. It's not the major obstacles and setbacks that impose the steepest toll, but the lesser-noticed, long-term effects sustained from repeated hits.

DEATH BY "LITTLE FOXES"

King Solomon, whose lands endured everything from invading armies to devastating droughts, wrote of the "little foxes that ruin the vineyards" (Song of Songs 2:15). I want to suggest four such "little foxes" common to church planters—seemingly small, repeating blows that may not feel debilitating individually, but whose cumulative effect takes as great a toll as any single punch you could endure.

1. Your best stuff is yawned at. You pour your greatest creative juices into designing a compelling resource or experience—a message series, a discipleship plan, a training retreat, an outreach event, a missional project. You're genuinely surprised when it receives only a tepid response. Within weeks, participation fizzles, or people simply don't engage at all.

The Old Testament prophets routinely experienced this reaction. No one led with more passion and conviction. No one communicated God's critical message more dynamically. Yet they were consistently disregarded and discredited, and their anointed messages were brushed off or ignored altogether (2 Chronicles 36:16). Jesus pointed to them when sorrowing over how his own representatives would be treated. Take heart, he said, when you're despised and rejected, "for that is how their ancestors treated the prophets" (Luke 6:23).

Your best work will regularly be met with shrugs and yawns. It will perplex you. Then it will annoy you. Eventually it will push you toward a victim mentality and drain your creative motivation. Why should you invest so much again when you already know the outcome will only leave you frustrated and disappointed?

2. Your people don't make progress. You set out fully believing that God will use you to make a significant difference in people's lives, confident their genuine God-encounters will result in crucial lifestyle changes and lessons learned. Then you hear how someone made a terrible choice just days after you taught on that very topic or counseled them clearly in the opposite direction. You see people who were long over a bad habit return to the exact same involvement. It's bad enough watching people drive over a cliff; it's far worse when they plow through the guardrails and road signs you've erected to keep them on course.

Proverbs 26:11 uses a vivid, if disgusting, word picture to describe the way of a fool: "As a dog returns to its vomit, so fools repeat their folly." Peter quotes that verse and adds another messy animal to the mix: "A sow that is washed returns to her wallowing in the mud" (2 Peter 2:22).

You know that kind of thing happens; you just don't think it will happen under your leadership. Until it does. Again and again.

There's an old Italian proverb that says, "People change . . . but not very much."[6] When you notice that to be true among *your* people, on *your* watch, it catches you off guard. When it continues repeatedly, the cumulative weight wears on your soul.

3. Your former attendees outnumber your current ones. This one sneaks up on you, because the first time you run into someone in public who tells you they attend your newly planted church, you feel a genuine thrill. But sooner or later, another "first time" follows, when you encounter someone who *used to* attend but no longer does. It creates an awkward moment. Do you approach them? Do you make small talk? Do you pretend not to see them?

Earlier I encouraged you not to spend time attempting to prevent defections. It's a futile pursuit. But that doesn't mean it won't take a toll on you when it happens. Many people who leave a church do so for less-than-godly reasons. If you stick around long enough, you'll stand a much better chance of running into someone who has come and left than someone who currently attends. You'll find yourself looking at the ground and avoiding eye contact when you're in public, for fear that you'll encounter yet another one.

4. You feel alone. You may be naturally gregarious, an extrovert who makes friends easily. Leadership will isolate you, nonetheless, because no one will be able to relate to the pressure you feel, the responsibility you carry, or the criticisms you absorb.

You'll decide you can't talk about such things with members of your body, because they count on you to be above the fray, to pull them up when *they're* discouraged, to rally them to charge forward in the face of opposition and attack. Besides, the people causing your greatest wounds will be fellow sheep in the flock, and you'll sense an obligation not to gossip or disparage one sheep to another. The more disappointments you encounter at your people's hands, the fewer other people you'll find with whom you can be completely transparent. You'll feel progressively more alone.

Retired general Colin Powell reserved this for last in his *18 Lessons in Leadership*. "Command is lonely," he said and then added, "Harry Truman was right. Whether you're a CEO or the temporary head of a project team, the buck stops here . . . Even as you create an informal, open, collaborative corporate culture, prepare to be lonely."[7]

One recent survey revealed that 58 percent of pastors do not have anyone in their lives they consider "a good true friend."[8] When you feel that intense loneliness, you'll be—dare I say it—not alone. The prophet Elijah, fresh off his greatest career victory over the prophets of Baal, descended into a deep loneliness. He withdrew, wished for death, and blurted to God, "I am the only one left" (1 Kings 19:10). God's revelation that Elijah actually wasn't—that seven thousand others hadn't bowed the knee to Baal—didn't change the fact that he felt that way.

Paul knew the growing isolation of leadership. He wrote to Timothy:

> Demas, because he loved this world, has deserted me and has gone to Thessalonica. Crescens has gone to Galatia, and Titus to Dalmatia . . .
>
> Alexander the metalworker did me a great deal of harm. The Lord will repay him for what he has done. You too should be on your guard against him, because he strongly opposed our message.
>
> At my first defense, no one came to my support, but everyone deserted me. May it not be held against them.
>
> 2 TIMOTHY 4:10, 14–16

Perception, it's said, is nine-tenths of reality. And leaders, though not entirely objective, ultimately perceive that no one in their world feels what they feel, understands them, or is willing to walk through the fire with them.

COLONEL JESSUP WAS RIGHT

Like Chinese water torture, the relentless drip-drip-drip of these disappointments amasses into a soul-crushing force. You'll be aware that often the very people who should be most grateful for your leadership and sacrifice are the ones criticizing your weaknesses and questioning your judgment. You'll feel justifiable anger over their ingratitude and presumption. And you'll come to the realization that, though he was demonized in the classic movie *A Few Good Men*, Jack Nicholson's Colonel Jessup character was mostly spot-on when he delivered his famous rant:

I have a greater responsibility than you can possibly fathom . . .

You don't want the truth, because deep down in places you don't talk about at parties, you want me on that wall. You need me on that wall . . .

I have neither the time nor the inclination to explain myself to a man who rises and sleeps under the blanket of the very freedom that I provide, and then questions the manner in which I provide it! I would rather you just said thank you and went on your way. Otherwise, I suggest you pick up a weapon and stand a post. Either way, I don't give a damn what you think you're entitled to![9]

You probably won't admit it to anyone, but you'll carry a similar sense of wounded, misunderstood superiority. It'll leave you feeling alone and victimized, unappreciated and angry. Equal parts sorrow and indignation.

PREVENTIVE MEDICINE

I believe the single most glaring weakness in the church planting world today is the lack of focus on the planter's holistic health. Addressing the leader's spiritual, emotional, and physical well-being has largely been relegated to recovery service for those who succumb to the pressure. At that point, they're viewed as poor weaklings for not being able to hack it. But every church planter inescapably deals with the exorbitant cost of leading, and we're fools not to give it proper attention.

Recognizing the price of leadership is a start. Installing preventive measures to mitigate its damage is even better. The good news is that very tangible, implementable instruments can be introduced to substantially reduce the number of leaders who crash and burn, or wither and die. I'll offer three I contend are so vital that you shouldn't accept a church planting leadership position, or commission someone for one, unless the package includes all three.

1. The essentiality of partnership. Flying solo is the stuff of movie heroes. "In a world . . . ," the Don LaFontaine-esque trailers dramatically announce, "one man stands alone to save the day." In the *real* world, however, lone wolves are the first to get picked off.

Small business start-ups launched as partnerships succeed at a rate four times greater than sole proprietorships. The statistics reinforce Scripture's precedent. When initiating efforts to take new territory in the name of Christ, God has consistently prescribed partnership.

Take a casual tour through the New Testament and you'll see a recurring pattern. Jesus dispatches the Twelve to spread the gospel message, sending them out in twos (Mark 6:7). He does the same when commissioning the Seventy-Two (Luke 10:1). Peter partners with John when preaching to the Jews (Acts 4). Paul and Barnabas are teamed to take the gospel to the Gentiles (Acts 13). Even when those two come to an impasse that leads to their separation, the first thing each does is find a new partner to accompany him on the next assignment (Acts 15:39–40).

God almost never sends church planters out alone.

I've come to the place where I'm "this close" to calling it unbiblical to plant a church solo. The drain on a leader is so intense, so demanding, that he desperately needs a partner (beyond his spouse) who eats, breathes, and sleeps it to the same degree he does.

I've experienced this difference firsthand. Having walked through the desolation of planting and failing once, I determined not to attempt it again unless I could seek out a willing partner. We slowly raised additional support toward that end (which was no small task), and eighteen months after our arrival to plant, Dan Burmeister joined me in the adventure.

Dan's partnership made all the difference in the world. I now had someone as deeply committed to our vision as me. When I staggered, I could draw on his strength as a channel of God's provision. When there were celebrative moments, he could rejoice with me to a level no one else could match. When we faced cross-roads and challenges, he talked me off the precipice more than once. I was able to do the same with him. I can honestly say I wouldn't have survived without the camaraderie and support I regularly received by having someone in the foxhole with me.

You need a true partner. Don't move forward until God provides one.

2. The essentiality of peer community. I have a pet peeve about ministeriums—those citywide gatherings where pastors meet in a show of ecumenical unity and engage in some combination of eating lunch, highlighting a social program, and quasi-encouraging each other over small talk and name-dropping. They frankly make my skin crawl. I've attended too many thinly veiled pissing contests where everyone is jockeying for position, humbly bragging about their accomplishments, and managing to work in casual mentions of their attendance numbers.

You don't need that. Nobody needs that.

But you do need a brotherhood of like-minded fellow warriors who fully understand what each other is going through and can bandage one another's wounds. When the disciples returned from their Jesus-commissioned, inaugural church planting assignment, the first thing he had them do was get away with each other to "get some rest" (Mark 6:31). Finding and maintaining that kind of outlet is perhaps the greatest gift you can give yourself as a leader.

I previously mentioned the group of church planters I sought out after having been beaten to a pulp in my first church planting attempt. From that gathering, four of us sensed a common bond and made a commitment to continue meeting monthly, solely for the purpose of supporting one another.

It may have been the best ministry decision I've ever made. Together, we pledged to pursue and value each other completely independently from how our churches were doing or what cool program we were trying. We promised to cut the crap and connect on a "How are you *really* doing?" level. We commiserated together—a lot. We ached with and for one another. We checked in on each other between meetings and sometimes just laughed at the absurdity of what every pastor experiences.

During the two decades that followed, one of our number suffered an emotional breakdown. Another of us lost his church and then his marriage. All of us dealt with children choosing paths that broke our hearts. We walked together through betrayals, criticisms, failures, aging, and, every now and then, something actually worth rejoicing over.

Because the foundation was true brotherhood and not "success," there wasn't a single time I remember feeling anything but joy when one of them reported a positive turn. It was an utterly different dynamic than anything I'd encountered with other pastors.

Twenty-five years later, only one of those four guys still leads the same church he was starting when we first met. Two of us have moved to different states, on opposite coasts. But we still meet every month via video. The one whose marriage ended found love again and now leads a cutting-edge ministry to addicts. We're all still hanging on to Jesus and attempting to serve him. We're older, sport less hair and more wrinkles, and pretty much owe each other our lives.

You need that for yourself. Not a supervisor, not a staff member, not your spouse. A band of brothers doing the same thing as you—the only ones on the planet who can fully understand the utter uniqueness of being the point leader of a church plant in your area. You don't have to explain yourself to them. They get it. They feel it. And they, like you, desperately need a place where they can be understood, or complain without anyone looking at them funny.

If such community doesn't exist around you, pray for God to lead you to a couple of like-minded brothers, and take the initiative to create one. You'll never regret it.

3. **The essentiality of intentional spiritual formation.** When churches and church planting networks vet potential planters, any group worth its salt lists mature, godly character as the absolute highest priority for its candidates. Above any skill set, they want to know that the person shepherding the flock is someone with an authentic, deep, mature level of spiritual health.

Once the vetting process is duly satisfied, however, many sending organizations never think about it again. Because "the best predictor of future behavior is past behavior," they make a holy assumption that the planter's spiritual formation is fully developed, and its ongoing maintenance is a matter of daily discipline they're confident the leader will sustain.

But you and I both know that church planters, like all pastors, walk through incredibly dry spiritual seasons. Our time with God becomes utilitarian—performed as a means to an end, whether it be message prep or because it's our professional duty. We lead almost every meeting we attend. We design God-encounters for others, but seldom are guided through one ourselves. We're always the mentor, never the mentee.

When pastors crash spectacularly, subsequent investigations almost always reveal a slow drift and disconnection from personal, ongoing spiritual formation. We're leading others, but no one is leading us, because it's assumed we can lead ourselves.

RECOVERY VERSUS PREVENTION

My friend Michael Bischof founded and directs SouLeader Resources, a ministry dedicated to empowering soul wholeness in pastors and leaders. He's often contacted after a moral failure or church leadership crisis, asked to come in and navigate disaster recovery for a church or its pastor. Someone has burned out; a hidden addiction has been revealed; an affair has ravaged a family and a church; dysfunctional leadership practices have created a toxic environment resulting in a church split. Michael's team is absolutely amazing at injecting healing processes and experiences into seemingly hopeless situations, rescuing many good men and women, their marriages, and their churches.

Michael has expressed his yearning to be involved earlier in the story, to help leaders address their soul's health before things go south. But he shared a troubling reality. Most leaders—and churches—don't see the need for the kinds of help he offers until the damage is already done. It's rare for a church to provide spiritual formation resources for its lead pastor. Pastors are *way* too busy to afford themselves the luxury of extended times of guided spiritual growth. We figure we're managing fine. And we don't see the connection between the lack of intentional spiritual formation and the slide into discouragement or deviant behavior.

That needs to change. In chapter 9, I encouraged you to pursue a spiritual director as part of your foundational self-care. Now I'll poke the bear further. If you want to stave off the crippling costs of derailed leadership, then you should embed overt, ongoing spiritual formation into your funding and schedule. Build it into your lifestyle and calendar. Dedicate times when you—and your team if you have one—are guided through spiritual exercises designed to perform heart-level procedures regularly on yourselves. Not self-surgery, but occasions when the scalpel is entrusted to gifted others who have no stake in your church or ministry, and who love you enough to use it.

The biggest objection I hear to this practice is that giving attention to the leader's spiritual development will divert time, money, and energy from the fields that are white for harvest. But which costs more, a couple thousand dollars a year devoted to a seemingly unnecessary, ancillary pastoral "perk," or the cost of discovering a pastor is well past burnout and facing debilitating depression? How about the price of emergency counseling after the revelation of a hidden lifestyle sin or marital crisis?

I urge every church planting project, from its very inception, to incorporate line items into its budget for pastoral spiritual health outlets every bit as much as it includes church planter assessment, start-up costs, and salary.

Few would disagree what a church needs most in its leader is a man who is hearing from God, close to God, and filled with God. It's what we look for, and what we strive to be. But it's time to stop assuming that simply getting the right guy will excuse us from having to worry about his ongoing spiritual health. He's an evolving, flesh-bound, weakened vessel, just as susceptible to spiritual atrophy as anyone he's shepherding. Perhaps he's even more susceptible, because everyone assumes he's the one person who doesn't need to be checked on or invested in. He does.

You do.

Leaders pay a high price for leading. The costs run deeper than anything we could have envisioned when we signed up for the job. But becoming fully aware of that price, and proactively investing in measures that maintain our perspective and health while enduring it, allows us a privileged position. We occupy front row seats to the most wondrous things God accomplishes on earth. We witness the transforming power of God's love to forever change lives, sometimes through our direct participation. We get to see the miraculous and touch the eternal.

And that is a payoff well worth the price.

CHAPTER 12

THE TRUTH ABOUT GOD'S ULTIMATE PLAN FOR YOUR CHURCH

or

Only God Knows, and He's Not Telling

Bait-and-Switch / *(bāt-ənd-swĭch)* / *noun*

1. "The action (generally illegal) of advertising goods that are an apparent bargain, with the intention of substituting inferior or more expensive goods."[1]
2. "The ploy of offering a person something desirable to gain favor, then thwarting expectations with something less desirable."[2]
3. What God does with the "vision" he gives church planters.

When we venture to plant a new church, vision—"a clear mental image of a preferable future"[3]—occupies center stage. Vision is what ignites the pioneering leader's drive and sustains them through challenges, setbacks, and roadblocks. Vision propels us forward to empower and enlist others to chase the dream—God's dream—together.

Which only serves to amplify our utter disillusionment when we discover one more truth few are ever told about church planting: God has little intention of fulfilling the vision he gives us in the form we receive it.

God, it seems, is a master of the bait-and-switch.

Now before that gets your boxers in a bunch, consider this: allowing people to embrace a vision they're convinced is from him and then taking it in directions he didn't mention to accomplish purposes he didn't disclose has always been God's MO.

YOU FAILED TO INCLUDE THAT LITTLE DETAIL

When God delivered the Israelite nation from bondage and promised them a land of their own, he led them on what turned out to be a forty-year forced march—circuitous wanderings through barren wasteland under severe conditions. They hung in there, mostly because they had no choice, but also because they carried a God-given vision of a land flowing with milk and honey on the other side of the journey (Exodus 3:8).

Those forty years were agonizing—filled with threat, vulnerability, and constant risk. The wanderers never felt settled or secure. The rations couldn't be stored. Basic resources were limited. And then there were the infrastructure issues. Have you ever thought about what the sewage system would look like for a nomadic group roughly comparable in population to greater Cleveland?

They were willing to endure for only one reason—the vision. Milk and honey.

Imagine their surprise when, after forty years of hardship, they were informed of a few small details about inheriting the land that had been conveniently left out of the initial vision:

- They would have to fight their way across the entirety of the country in order to claim it.
- The opposing armies included hulking warrior-giants.
- The free Daily Manna Bar was now closed.
- Oh, and the milk and honey thing? That was just a metaphor. The land was fertile and all, but they would find no *actual* milk or honey flowing through Palestine.
- And one more nugget. Yes, reaching the Promised Land was important, but the underlying reason for all the wandering hadn't been primarily to reach a destination. It was to teach some heart lessons along the way. More on that later.

Bottom line? Reality was going to look much different from the vision they'd been driven by for four decades. God advertised one picture and then delivered another. It's a technique he's regularly employed ever since.

Just a few further samples.

Joseph's rise. Joseph received a dazzling vision—sun and moon and stars, along with his eleven brothers, bowing down to him (Genesis 37:5–11). What he experienced included being conspired against, sold into slavery, and accused of capital crimes (Genesis 37–39). He rotted in a forgotten prison for a good long time. It seems those scenes had been omitted from the movie trailer.

The Great Commission. Jesus imparted the vision of the Great Commission as a Spirit-empowered, worldwide victory tour to spread the gospel (Acts 1:8). The apostles were sent with a promise of Jesus' uninterrupted presence (Matthew 28:20), and to whatever extent we can trust the authenticity of the gospel of Mark's longer ending, such power displays as demon exorcism, divine healing, and protection from the effects of deadly poison (Mark 16:15–18). But though he'd earlier hinted things wouldn't always be easy, Jesus' grand assignment didn't fully disclose the constant opposition, beatings, imprisonments, and eventual martyrdom for ten of the eleven apostles who received the commission.

Paul's Macedonian call. When Paul received his Macedonian vision, all he saw was a man begging him to "come over to Macedonia and help us" (Acts 16:9), a fairly innocuous request. Paul headed west, assuming his assignment was to "help." What awaited him was pain. He would be run out of town, beaten to within an inch of his life, stoned and left for dead, rejected and dogged by opposition. Some of the churches Paul planted would face annihilation to such an extent that he'd have reason to doubt they'd still be in existence when he received later status reports. He probably never even got to meet the guy in his vision.

And then there's you. God gives you a vision. It's pure, lucid, and undeniable. It's kingdom-focused and multitude-of-counselors affirmed. You see it so clearly and believe in it so deeply that nothing could sway you from your commitment to follow God to its fulfillment.

But as the story unfolds, major twists and radical turns create significant deviations from the original picture. You try to course-correct, to maintain the path toward the image you're convinced is God's will. But the most attractive elements of the vision never materialize. Crowd sizes, baptism numbers, the spirit and tone of a thriving gospel outpost, the expansion of a unified team? No-shows. By the time you're too far down the road to turn back, the result is light years removed from your initial vision. You're left feeling confused and deeply disappointed, questioning whether you misinterpreted the vision in the first place, somehow failed to deliver it, or, worse, were duped by God about it.

If you decide it was that last possibility, you'll want to call shenanigans. How can the God who is Truth draw a blueprint for something he doesn't intend to build? How can he justify allowing you to feel absolutely convinced he's steering your ship toward a particular port, knowing all along he's planning to land you on an entirely different island? What kind of God does that to those who have completely committed themselves to take him at his word?

THE TRUTH ABOUT VISION

The answer emerges from a combination of several revelations about the nature of vision and about God's purposes for giving it.[4] The sooner we can grasp these, the better we'll embrace the fact that our outcomes not only can but *must* differ from our vision, for good reason.

1. **Vision is more about the journey than the destination.** After a lifetime of trying to convince myself otherwise, I finally had to admit something: I'm a destination guy.

I know, I know, "Life is about the journey, not the destination." I agree that's how I *should* feel; it just isn't what I *actually* feel.

My wife, Marcia, is a "journey" person. She loves long walks and leisurely bike rides. She doesn't need them to lead anywhere in particular; she savors being out on paths and trails, breathing in the beauty of nature and the wonder that God brings along the way.

I agree to walk and bike with her because I love her. But I just don't get it. My personality wants to know where the road is going, and how to get there as swiftly as possible. I don't understand walking around without a task to accomplish or a destination to reach. Now, if there's an ice cream shop a few miles away and I know the bike ride will ultimately take me there, I'm all in. That reward makes the effort worthwhile. But to go around in circles for the pure joy of seeing the same sights I've already seen a hundred times? I appreciate those who embrace the poetry found in that; I'm simply not wired that way.

I admit that's incredibly shallow. I'm not proud of it. But for myself and many leaders like me, the journey is little more than flyover country serving only to slow us down on the way to the destination.

This makes for a difficult lesson because, in God's design, vision is far more about what happens on the journey than about ever reaching a destination. He shows us a picture to move us in a general direction and then introduces unforetold elements to accomplish purposes he considers more important than reaching a specific location.

"Go from your country . . . to the land I will show you," God commanded Abraham (Genesis 12:1). God painted a verbal picture for Abraham: He would father great nations, see his name lauded, be a blessing to all peoples on earth who would be blessed through him. Spectacular stuff. The vision ignited his passion, courage, and actions. But Abraham never saw the fulfillment of his vision. At least not in his lifetime.

He was never meant to. What God accomplished in the journey was always the greater focus. God moved through Abraham's travels to enact purposes he didn't disclose in advance: to change Abraham's heart, to position his line, to create a path for the Messiah's coming. Abraham followed the vision "by faith . . . even though he did not know where he was going" (Hebrews 11:8). He became one of many the writer of Hebrews would describe as "still living by faith when they died. They did not receive the things promised; they only saw them and welcomed them from a distance" (Hebrews 11:13).

Vision serves an essential purpose. It just isn't to precisely produce the image we see when it's given.

2. Vision imparts a merciful naivete. First-time parents possess what we might call a "merciful naivete" about child-rearing. Captivated by a vision filled with hope and wonder, they anticipate the thrill of bringing a sweet child into a loving home, investing positive qualities into him or her, and delighting in the magic of their discovery and development. After all, the two words they've always heard associated with children are "pride" and "joy."

Thankfully, they're prevented from seeing the full picture of what awaits them. The bloodcurdling screams of colic, the diaper blowouts, the terrible twos, and threes, and sixteens. The life-sucking sacrifices, heartaches, and betrayals almost all parents endure while attempting to guide their children safely to adulthood. After it's all said and done, most parents declare they'd do it again if given the choice. But if young couples were granted full disclosure of the price they were about to pay, a whole heck of a lot less children would be brought into this world.

If God had shown Moses, Joseph, or Paul the entire scope of what lay ahead, we're left to speculate how motivated they would have been to accept their assignments. Their vision afforded them a merciful naivete, enough to motivate and mobilize them, but not exhaustive enough to scare them off.

Your vision serves the same purpose. The mental image God bestows graciously draws you into privileged participation in a journey you won't regret when it's done, but one that you might not have been willing to enter if you had known the entire plan in advance.

3. Vision is subject to glory preservation. Sunlight has been called the human body's best friend and worst enemy. Direct exposure to sunlight triggers production of vitamin D, which protects against inflammation, lowers high blood pressure, and strengthens muscle tissue.[5] Students who have been in the sun score better on tests.[6] And there is evidence to support sunlight's role in preventing breast cancer, colon cancer, prostate cancer, ovarian cancer, heart disease, multiple sclerosis, and osteoporosis.[7]

But ultraviolet radiation from the same sunlight, as the world has been made well aware, can also cause permanent retinal damage, premature aging, and multiple types of cancer. Sunlight blesses us, but too much exposure can do irreparable damage.

Human achievement carries similar dual effects, especially when performed in spiritual endeavors. Being used to carry out God-assignments is one of life's greatest thrills. But it also produces "glory"—elevated praise and honor, the "credit" for accomplishment and its accompanying splendor. Glory is intrinsic to God's nature, but toxic to preresurrected humans.[8] When we pursue and complete a God-given vision, we're susceptible to absorbing the glory it produces rather than redirecting it toward its rightful recipient.

Full Vision Achievement: A Spiritual Carcinogen

The director of a nonprofit ministry championed his newest vision to create a program for the underserved. On the organization's website, he conveyed the basis for his confidence that the dream would become reality:

> God gave me a vision for a church and we built it!
> God gave me a vision for a preschool and we built it.
> God gave me a vision for an afterschool program and we built it.
> God gave me a vision to start a van/food connection for the hungry and we built it.
> Now God has led me to start a new parachurch ministry.

That probably strikes you the same way it does me.

You may sincerely believe you'll respond differently when you carry out the vision that God gave you. You'll give him all the glory he rightfully deserves, and you'll reject any credit directed your way. But our flesh entices us otherwise. Glory is seductive, addictive, and deadly. And because he loves us, God mercifully installs protective measures to guard against our ingesting its carcinogens.

This is essentially what was going on when Paul wrote these familiar words: "In order to keep me from becoming conceited, I was given a thorn in my flesh" (2 Corinthians 12:7). It's almost comical how much effort has gone into speculating what exactly Paul's "thorn" was. Was it an eyesight problem? Intestinal issues? False teachers? Demon oppression?

It doesn't matter. The point is, God chooses to use human beings to accomplish his purposes, but he also knows that when they achieve their goals, they're susceptible to absorbing the glory it produces. So he protects us from ourselves. The "King of glory" uses a variety of methods to do so, but chief among them is preventing the entirety of the vision he's given to be completed by our efforts.

Let's return for a moment to Deuteronomy 8, and the bait-and-switch vision of entering the Promised Land. God cautioned his people that the greatest danger they would face would not be the giants inhabiting the land; it would be the risk of realizing their vision and believing they were responsible for doing so.

> When your herds and flocks grow large and your silver and gold increase and all you have is multiplied, then your heart will become proud and you will forget the LORD your God, who brought you out of Egypt, out of the land of slavery. He led you through the vast and dreadful desert, that thirsty and waterless land, with its venomous snakes and scorpions. He brought you water out of hard rock. He gave you manna

to eat in the wilderness, something your ancestors had never known, to humble and test you so that in the end it might go well with you. You may say to yourself, "My power and the strength of my hands have produced this wealth for me." But remember the LORD your God, for it is he who gives you the ability to produce wealth, and so confirms his covenant, which he swore to your ancestors, as it is today.

DEUTERONOMY 8:13–18

God has favored you by granting you the chance to pursue an eternity-affecting vision on his behalf. He's favored you even further by not allowing you to fully achieve it.

4. Vision sets the stage for God to accomplish his sovereign will. The ultimate plan behind everything God is doing on earth has been called his "sovereign will." Scripture describes it as his "eternal purpose" (Ephesians 3:11), held exclusively in the mind of the Eternal One and beyond any human capacity to fathom or comprehend.

Garry Friesen, in the best book I've ever seen on the subject—*Decision Making and the Will of God*—offers these characteristics of God's sovereign will:

- **Certain**—it will be fulfilled
- **Detailed**—includes all things
- **Hidden**—except when revealed by prophecy[9]

That last point is significant. Because his ultimate will remains the exclusive domain of the Almighty, he bears no obligation to explain it, defend it, or divulge it. In fact, he ensures it remains outside our knowledge in the moment. Friesen writes, "God's plan . . . is *hidden*. Older theologians often referred to God's sovereign will as His 'secret will,' in contrast to His revealed will in the Bible. God hides His sovereign will until it happens. Curl up with a good history book on a rainy day and you are reading God's sovereign will for the past. Would you like to know God's sovereign will for next Tuesday? Wait until next Wednesday. Only God knows what will happen in advance, and He's not telling."[10]

In real-life terms, this means we can be reasonably sure that what we're convinced is God's will for our endeavors nowhere approaches his actual, ultimate purpose. God allows us to see and pursue a vision we correctly understand comes from him, but he retains a distinct, hidden purpose behind it—a superior, certain one. "In their hearts humans plan their course, but the LORD establishes their steps," Scripture reminds us (Proverbs 16:9). Only God knows what that plan actually is. And he's not telling.

It's not only possible, but it's entirely likely God is doing that with your church plant.

What if God's entire purpose behind your vision to plant a church is to accomplish something that has nothing to do with you? What if the whole endeavor is actually about a singular experience he intends for someone in your core group? What if his solitary reason for moving you where you are is to position one of your children to meet and marry someone they wouldn't have otherwise, to accomplish something through one of their grandchildren two generations away? What if everything you're sacrificing your life to pursue is part of a plan to effectuate other kingdom goals in other places, among other people, none of which you will live to see?

Here are the big questions:

- If you know God has never intended, nor feels obligated, to produce the vision you believe he has embedded within you, will you still sign up for it?

- Can you release your demand that God deliver what you've assumed he promised you, on the basis of the fact he is God and you are not?
- Can you accept the idea that he has a will he's enacting but isn't divulging, and that he doesn't owe you explanations or outcomes?
- Will you sell out to God's ultimate vision, even if you know it won't match the one you currently see?

Please hear this: in the end, no one who fully and completely answers yes to these questions will ever regret it.

THE QUINTESSENTIAL BAIT-AND-SWITCH

Joseph declared to his brothers that the evil plans they'd conceived, and his own bold visions, fell servant to another plan that God always had in mind. His famous words, "God intended it for good" (Genesis 50:20), stamped God's trademark on every vision to follow. The final picture of God's completed plan always surpasses whatever vision we might have clung to.

Your efforts to plant a church—with all its path shifts, frustrations, and disappointments—will prove just as eternally worthwhile. Romans 8:28 may be overly quoted, but that doesn't make it any less true. The God you serve is good. He's in control. He will prevail. Every death of a dream, every divergence from the goal, every sacrifice and failure you endure, will ultimately be swallowed up by the victory of God's unfurled master plan—his magnum opus—accomplished through you in ways you never, ever saw coming.

When this great adventure is complete, we'll stand before his throne, cast whatever crowns he's awarded back at his feet, bow in worship, and erupt in applause at the genius and generosity of the Most High God. He'll have done more marvelous things than we could ever have imagined and will have allowed us the honor of being co-journeyers on the greatest adventure the world has ever known.

That is a vision worth surrendering everything for.

EPILOGUE

The band of church planting brothers I mentioned in chapter 11—who became my lifelines, sanctuary, and fraternity—once made a pact. Because we'd learned there is no such thing as an "expert" in real-life ministry—that everybody is writing their own unique story and making it up as they go along—we were all forbidden to ever write a book.

When someone authors a book, the presumption is that they know something others don't. They've somehow mastered a topic so thoroughly that people should be willing to pay good money to learn from them. We all knew that would never be true of us, so we made a vow: if any of us ever attempted to write a book, the others had permission to hunt him down and whack him with baseball bats.

I seriously considered writing the book you've just read under a pseudonym solely to avoid that pummeling. The publisher wouldn't let me, so now I'm watching my back and waiting for ambushes.

But I broke the pact, knowing what I hope you've been able to sense: I didn't put pen to paper here under the pretense of having anything to emulate. I did it to throw a life preserver to people who I know are struggling and working their tails off, many of them floundering and suffering silently, wondering what's wrong or what they're missing. It's an attempt to outshout the noise and say what they desperately need to hear: You're not crazy. You're not inferior. And you're not alone.

If just that much can somehow penetrate to the heart of my brothers and sisters doing the hardest, most significant work on earth, then writing these pages will be worth the impending thrashing.

To those currently church planting or considering doing so, let me add this. If I could rub a genie's lamp and be granted three wishes, I'd be tempted to instantly make every church planter who is proclaiming the uncompromised message of salvation through Jesus Christ wildly successful. But rather, I think I might use my wishes to grant you some "permissions" instead.

I'd grant you permission to be honest *with yourself*. To acknowledge that you're weary, insecure, or disillusioned. To admit you're really messed up, full of conflicting motives and selfishness blended with a sincere desire to honor God and depopulate hell. But to know there's not something inherently wrong with you when you fight dark thoughts and feel the tsunami of doubt. And to know that your Father in heaven feels it with you and genuinely, truly holds tightly to you even in your ugliest moments.

I'd grant you permission to be honest *with God*. To go toe-to-toe with him over your anger, your frustration, and your disappointment—even disappointment with him. To know he can handle it and actually welcomes it without repercussion. To rest in your absolute security in him, knowing he's not going to strip you of his favor just because you're frayed at the edges and capable of being extraordinarily mad at him at the exact same moment you love him with everything you've got.

And I'd grant you permission to know, *really know*, deep in the fabric of your soul, just how much of a rock star God actually considers you to be. Not because of your superior gifts or dynamic personality, not because of your numerical growth or proven results, but simply because you are his. Cherished. Celebrated. Bearing the stamp, "Beloved."

You're serving the greatest cause, and the greatest Master, in the universe. And when the story is written and the adventure is told, you're going to hear the words, "Well done, good and faithful servant," from the lips that matter most.

May your tribe increase.

ACKNOWLEDGMENTS

Anyone who is granted a platform for influence stands on the shoulders of countless others without whose contributions they never would have reached that position. I'm no exception. Over multiple decades, an army of God-loving people has invested in, uplifted, persevered with, and shielded me so thoroughly that they could easily be credited as coauthors of this book.

My parents, Tom and Nancy Bennardo, not only gave me life and steered me toward Christ, but they have believed in me and prayed unceasingly for me from my earliest steps into ministry.

An all-star lineup of peers and mentors have shaped my heart in ways that continue to bear fruit in incalculable ways. Don Roth saw something worth reclaiming in me when no one else was looking anymore. Longtime friend and fellow church planter Dave McClellan was the first to name and confess our mutual "Destined for Greatness" disease. We've been seeking recovery together ever since. My "brother from another mother," Steve Adriansen, has walked step-by-step with me through the adventure of ministry and life; he may be the wisest and most gracious man on the planet.

My "brother from the same mother," Mark Bennardo, has been both my best earthly friend and my source of sanity in ways only he can fully understand. His own church planting experience led him to coin the phrase I shamelessly ripped off: "People stayed away in droves." Don't tell him I said it, but he's far and away the more talented of the Bennardo boys. More importantly, the incomparable, holy way he cared for his wife, Tammy, through her twelve-year journey toward heaven stands as the single greatest source of inspiration in my life.

The body of Christ at Glendale Community Church and the family and staff at Life Community Church—especially Dan Burmeister, Larry Ely, J. R. Kennedy, and Rick and Sheila Tawney—served as the unwitting petri dishes for most of the lessons learned in these pages. They hung with me through the highest highs and lowest lows, and I'll forever be grateful for the privilege of leading them as we chased the dream of "redefining 'church' for this generation."

My colleagues at the Fellowship of Evangelical Churches and the Synergy Church Planting Network make up the healthiest church planting organization I've ever seen. I'm incredibly proud to serve alongside them. Rocky Rocholl, Scott Wagoner, Jay Nickless, Hal Lehman, Nate Zimmerman, Eric Hall, and Sloane Gerbers—thank you for living out the principles in this book. I'd stack you up anywhere against any team dedicated to expanding the kingdom of Jesus.

I'm deeply indebted to Larry Osborne, who not only graciously agreed to write the foreword but stepped up to say a guy with zero national name recognition had something worth hearing and then paved the way for it to be heard. Ryan Pazdur and the team from Zondervan believed in this project and contributed their considerable collective skills and clout to make the end product far better than its original and to create the platform for getting it out.

And then there's Greg Burlile, Phil Shomo, and Tim Tabor, who together form the "Fab Four" of fellow church planters I mention multiple times in the book. There is no way I can overstate the role that this fraternity has played in my life. So much of what you read in these pages emerged out of our shared experiences and brutally honest interactions. Guys, I'll be praising the Father forever for how he manifested himself to me through you. Please be gentle with the baseball bats.

I've been shaped into the man I am largely by the privilege of being a father to daughters. Lauren and Lindsey have been God's instruments in ways they'll never fully comprehend to make me more into their heavenly Father's image. Girls, if they hollowed out the moon, filled it with every daughter in the world, and let me pick whichever ones I wanted to be mine, I would choose . . . you.

When my wife, Marcia, first found me, I was a loud and proud Italian with a propensity for making every conversation about myself and a fashion style stuck in the 1970s. Her gentle but relentless refinements became God's greatest instruments in my "becoming." She's been my soul mate, partner, cheerleader, chief discipler, love of my life, and by far my greatest picture of God's character and grace for more than thirty-five years. Marsh, with you "I've got sunshine on a cloudy day," so "let's stay together," because "I only have eyes for you."

Finally—and at the risk of sounding like I'm saying it because everyone is supposed to—I need to lay every bit of honor at the feet of my risen, present, glorious Savior, Jesus Christ. I'm only beginning to grasp the incomprehensible depth of his grace and affection, his astonishing sacrifice in my place, and his furious love not just for the world but for me as the most undeserving of all sinners. Ultimately, I write, love, and live for an audience of One. To him belongs all the glory and praise forever.

NOTES

Chapter 1: The Truth about You

1. George Barna, *Leaders on Leadership* (Ventura, CA: Regal, 1997), 20.
2. Gary L. McIntosh and Samuel D. Rima Sr., *Overcoming the Dark Side of Leadership* (Grand Rapids: Baker, 1997).
3. Not unsurprisingly, a recent study found more than 31 percent of ordained pastors scored in the diagnostic range for "Narcissistic Personality Disorder" (see Darrell Puls, "Let Us Prey: The Frequency of Narcissistic Personality Disorder in Pastors," American Association of Christian Counselors, December 11, 2017, www.aacc.net/2017/12/11/let-us-prey-the-frequency-of-narcissistic-personality-disorder-in-pastors.
4. Gordon Livingston, *Too Soon Old, Too Late Smart: Thirty True Things You Need to Know Now* (Boston: Da Capo, 2009), 49.
5. *Men in Black*, directed by Barry Sonnenfeld, screenplay by Ed Solomon (Columbia Pictures, July 2, 1997).
6. A. W. Tozer, *The Root of Righteousness* (Chicago: Moody, 2015), 165.
7. Brennan Manning, *The Ragamuffin Gospel* (Sisters, OR: Multnomah, 1990), 164.
8. Jon Bloom, "When God Seems Silent," July 18, 2014, www.desiringgod.org/articles/when-god-seems-silent.
9. Larry Crabb, *Shattered Dreams* (Colorado Springs: WaterBrook, 2001), 157.

10. Henri J.M. Nouwen, *The Wounded Healer* (New York: Doubleday, 1972), 87.

Chapter 2: The Truth about "Proven" Methods

1. Chris Wadsworth, "How Understanding Retail Store Traffic Flow Can Improve Conversion," October 20, 2014, www.trafsys.com/how -understanding-retail-store-traffic-flow-can-improve-conversion.
2. Paco Underhill, *Why We Buy: The Science of Shopping* (New York: Simon & Schuster, 2009), 78.
3. Underhill, *Why We Buy*, 47.
4. "Paco Underhill Quotes," www.morefamousquotes.com/authors/ paco-underhill-quotes.
5. James Altucher, "Should the Answers on Quora Be Categorized into Experts' Opinion and Laymans' Opinion?" October 8, 2014, www.quora.com/Should-the-answers-on-Quora-be-categorized -into-experts-opinion-and-laymans-opinion.
6. *The Lord of the Rings: The Fellowship of the Ring*, directed by Peter Jackson, novel by J. R. R. Tolkien, screenplay by Fran Walsh (New Line Cinema, December 19, 2001).
7. Quoted in Mike Berardino, "Mike Tyson Explains One of His Famous Quotes," *Sun Sentinel*, November 9, 2012, www.sun -sentinel.com/sports/fl-xpm-2012-11-09-sfl-mike-tyson-explains -one-of-his-most-famous-quotes-20121109-story.html.
8. C. S. Lewis, *Prince Caspian* (1951; repr., New York: HarperCollins, 1994), 143.

Chapter 3: The Truth about Getting "Butts in Seats"

1. *Tim Allen Rewires America*, Showtime television special, December 7, 1991.
2. Nicholas Eberstadt, *A Nation of Takers: America's Entitlement Epidemic* (West Conshohocken, PA: Templeton Press, 2012), 80.
3. John Piper, "O Lord, Open a Door for the Word!" 1989, www .desiringgod.org/messages/o-lord-open-a-door-for-the-word.
4. Tom Mercer, *8 to 15: The World Is Smaller Than You Think* (Victorville, CA: Oikos, 2013).

Chapter 4: The Truth about Core Groups and Launch Teams

1. J. D. Greear, *Gaining by Losing: Why the Future Belongs to Churches That Send* (Grand Rapids: Zondervan, 2015), 112, 116.
2. "I've Done Everything for You," words and lyrics by Sammy Hagar, recorded by Rick Springfield, *Working Class Dog*, RCA Records, 1981.
3. *The Princess Bride*, directed by Rob Reiner, screenplay by William Goldman (Twentieth Century Fox, October 9, 1987).

Chapter 5: The Truth about the Back Door

1. William D. Hendricks, *Exit Interviews: Revealing Stories of Why People Are Leaving the Church* (Chicago: Moody, 1993), 10.
2. "Opportunity Cost," www.businessdictionary.com/definition/opportunity-cost.html.
3. David Murray, "Sheep: 'This Time It's Personal,'" January 5, 2011, http://headhearthand.org/blog/2011/01/05/sheep-this-time-its-personal.
4. "Herm Edwards: You Play to Win the Game," www.youtube.com/watch?v=AK7fEjrqabg.
5. C. S. Lewis, *The Last Battle* (1950; repr., New York: Harper Collins, 1994), 181.

Chapter 6: The Truth about "Lottery Winners"

1. Chris Morris, "7 Things That Are More Likely to Happen Than You Winning Powerball," *Fortune*, January 4, 2018, http://fortune.com/2018/01/04/powerball-number-odds.
2. https://en.wikipedia.org/wiki/Sotos_syndrome.
3. Cited by Greg Laurie, "Church Growth: When Communers Become Consumers," *Christian Post*, March 8, 2015, www.christianpost.com/news/church-growth-when-communers-become-consumers-135321.
4. Mike Breen, "Obituary for the American Church," *Mission Frontiers*, July 1, 2012, www.missionfrontiers.org/issue/article/obituary-for-the-american-church.

5. Joel Owens Rainey, "A Comparison of the Effectiveness of Selected Church Planting Models Measured by Conversion Growth and New Church Starts," EdD dissertation (Louisville, KY: Southern Baptist Theological Seminary, 2005), quoted in Edward Stetzer and Warren Bird, "The State of Church Planting in the United States: Research Overview and Qualitative Study of Primary Church Planting Entities" (Dallas, TX: Leadership Network, 2009), 11, www.christianitytoday.com/edstetzer/2009/january/state-of-church-planting.html.

6. Eugene Peterson, *The Pastor: A Memoir* (New York: HarperOne, 2011), 112.

7. Peterson, *The Pastor*, 4.

8. See J. R. Briggs, "Epic Fail," CT Pastors, Winter 2012, www.christianitytoday.com/pastors/2012/winter/epicfail.html.

9. Gene Edwards, *A Tale of Three Kings: A Study in Brokenness* (1980; repr., Wheaton, IL: Tyndale, 1992), 42.

10. Edwards, *Tale of Three Kings*, 40, italics original.

Chapter 7: The Truth about Pace

1. "Saturday Night in Toledo, Ohio," words and music by Randy Sparks, recorded by John Denver, *An Evening with John Denver*, RCA Records, 1975.

2. C. H. Spurgeon, "Go in Peace," sermon delivered at Metropolitan Tabernacle, Newington, England, September 28, 1883, http://archive.spurgeon.org/sermons/2770.php.

3. Kosuke Koyama, *Three Mile an Hour God: Biblical Reflections* (London: SCM, 1979), 6–7.

4. N. T. Wright, *After You Believe: Why Christian Character Matters* (New York: HarperOne, 2010), 3, italics original.

5. Quoted in Dorothy M. Stewart, ed., *The Westminster Collection of Christian Prayers* (Louisville: Westminster John Knox, 2002), 341.

6. Cited in John Ortberg, *The Life You've Always Wanted: Spiritual Disciplines for Ordinary People* (1997; repr., Grand Rapids: Zondervan, 2002), 76.

7. Cited in Ben Forer, "Divorce Drops, Long-Lasting Marriages Rise: U.S. Census Report," May 19, 2011, http://abcnews.go

.com/US/long-lasting-marriages-rise-us-census-report/story?id=
13638606.

Chapter 8: The Truth about "Church Multiplication Movements"

1. "Revolution," words and lyrics by John Lennon and Paul McCartney, recorded by The Beatles, *White Album*, Apple Records, 1968.
2. Derek Sivers, "How to Start a Movement," TED 2010, www.ted .com/talks/derek_sivers_how_to_start_a_movement.
3. Ed Stetzer and Warren Bird, *Viral Churches: Helping Church Planters Become Movement Makers* (San Francisco: Jossey-Bass, 2010), 116.
4. Max Lucado, *On the Anvil* (1985; repr., Carol Stream, IL: Tyndale, 2008), 120.
5. "Thought of the Day," *The Herald* (South Africa), April 5, 2017, www.pressreader.com/south-africa/the-herald-south-africa/20170 405/281865823320856.
6. Scott Goodson, "How to Spark a Movement," April 19, 2013, www.forbes.com/sites/marketshare/2013/04/19/how-to-spark-a -movement/#6505caa24eb1.
7. Patrick Morley, "Ten Characteristics of Revivals," 2010, www .maninthemirror.org/weekly-briefing/ten-characteristics -of-revivals.

Chapter 9: The Truth about How You're Viewed

1. Malcolm Gladwell, *Outliers* (Boston: Little, Brown & Co., 2008).
2. Brad Brisco, "Bivocational Church Planting: ReThinking It," November 11, 2016, www.namb.net/send-network-blog/rethinking -bivocational-church-planting.
3. *Black Christmas*, directed by Bob Clark, screenplay by Roy Moore (Warner Bros., December 20, 1974).
4. Brennan Manning, *The Furious Longing of God* (Colorado Springs: Cook, 2009), 35.
5. Brennan Manning, *Abba's Child: The Cry of the Heart for Intimate Belonging* (Colorado Springs: NavPress, 1994), 64–65, italics original.

Chapter 10: The Truth about "Excellence"

1. "Magic Kingdom Facts," Ron and Marie's Disney Trivia, www
   .disneytrivia.net/park_pages/wdw_mk_facts.php.
2. Quoted in Andy Meek, "Former Executive Shares the Secrets
   to How Disney Runs Its Empire," January 26, 2015, www
   .fastcompany.com/3041284/former-executive-shares-the-secrets
   -to-how-disney-runs-its-empire.
3. Years 1945–2005: Evan Comen, "The Size of a Home the Year
   You Were Born," May 25, 2016, https://247wallst.com/special
   -report/2016/05/25/the-size-of-a-home-the-year-you-were
   -born/. Year 2015: "Average Size of Floor Area in New Single
   -Family Homes Built for Sale in the United States from 1975
   to 2017 (in Square Feet)," www.statista.com/statistics/529371/
   floor-area-size-new-single-family-homes-usa.
4. Skye Jethani, "How Churches Became Cruise Ships," https://
   skyejethani.com/how-churches-became-cruise-ships.
5. Jethani, "How Churches Became Cruise Ships."
6. Terry Orlick, *In Pursuit of Excellence*, 5th ed. (1980; repr.,
   Champaign, IL: Human Kinetics, 2016).
7. I should note that the pendulum has swung in recent years, as
   those reacting to the pressure of expectations have championed
   "simple church" and "organic church" principles. But even in those
   circles, the base paradigm continues to assume that a significant
   list of activities and resources must be present for a church to
   consider itself ready to fulfill its purpose. "Simple churches" still
   feel the need to provide high-quality experiences for children,
   adept musicians, solid discipleship processes, intentional outreach
   outlets, and an ongoing list of obligatory services. Those that
   don't often experience a reduced half-life.
8. Larry Osborne, *Sticky Teams: Keeping Your Leadership Team and
   Staff on the Same Page* (Grand Rapids: Zondervan, 2010), 111–12.
9. Gary Keller, *The One Thing: The Surprisingly Simple Truth Behind
   Extraordinary Results* (Austin, TX: Bard, 2012), 46.
10. Keller, *One Thing*, 193.
11. Keller, *One Thing*, 10.

12. Keller, *One Thing*, 16.
13. Robert Fritz, *Creating* (New York: Ballantine, 1991), 76.

Chapter 11: The Truth about Leadership

1. Cited in D. J. Chuang, "What Peter Drucker Said about Pastors and Churches," June 12, 2014, http://djchuang.com/2014/peter-drucker -said-pastors-churches; Dan Chun, "Pastors Often Succumb to Job Burnout Due to Stress, Low Pay," November 18, 2006, http://the .honoluluadvertiser.com/article/2006/Nov/18/il/FP611180330.html.
2. Lisa Cannon Green, "Despite Stresses, Few Pastors Give Up on Ministry," September 1, 2015, https:/lifewayresearch.com/ 2015/09/01/despite-stresses-few-pastors-give-up-on-ministry.
3. Cited in H. B. London Jr. and Neil B. Wiseman, *Pastors at Greater Risk: Real Help from Pastors Who've Been There* (Ventura, CA: Regal, 2003), 86.
4. See Chad A. Tagge et al., "Concussion, Microvascular Injury, and Early Tauopathy in Young Athletes After Impact Head Injury and an Impact Concussion Mouse Model," *Brain: A Journal of Neurology* 141, no. 2 (February 2018): 422–58, https://academic .oup.com/brain/article/141/2/422/4815697.
5. Quoted in Cindy Boren, "A New Study Shows That Hits to the Head, Not Concussions, Cause CTE," January 18, 2018, www .washingtonpost.com/news/early-lead/wp/2018/01/18/a-new -study-shows-that-hits-to-the-head-not-concussions-cause-cte.
6. Okay, it's not Italian, but our people have a long history of claiming that all the best stuff originated with us, so why stop now?
7. Briefing presented by General Colin Powell to the Outreach to America Program, Sears Corporate Headquarters, Chicago, November 11, 2011, www.au.af.mil/au/afri/aspj/apjinternational/ apj-s/2011/2011-4/2011_4_02_powell_s_eng.pdf.
8. Francis A. Schaeffer Institute of Church Leadership Development, "Statistics on Pastors: 2016 Update," https://files .stablerack.com/webfiles/71795/pastorsstatWP2016.pdf.
9. *A Few Good Men*, directed by Rob Reiner, screenplay by Aaron Sorkin (Columbia Pictures, December 9, 1992).

Chapter 12: The Truth about God's Ultimate Plan for Your Church

1. "Bait-and-Switch," Oxford *Living* Dictionaries, https://en.oxford dictionaries.com/definition/bait-and-switch.

2. "Bait and Switch," Merriam-Webster Dictionary, www.merriam -webster.com/dictionary/bait%20and%20switch.

3. George Barna, *The Power of Vision: Discover and Apply God's Plan for Your Life and Ministry* (1992; repr., Grand Rapids: Baker, 2009), 28.

4. When speaking of "vision" here, I'm referring to what I'll call lowercase "v" vision—the kind that leaders see in their minds' eye without claims of being a God-appointed prophet. This is the far more common type of vision that God grants, in contrast to uppercase "V" visions given to the prophets, which are very specific, very literal, and very much fulfilled to the letter, though still often not fully understood at the time of their giving. Most church planters would not claim to have received uppercase "V" vision of a biblical prophet, but their picture is one they believe comes from God nonetheless.

5. See Nicole Dossantos, "15 Health Benefits of Sunshine," April 27, 2016, www.theactivetimes.com/fitness/nutrition/15-health -benefits-sunshine.

6. See Jennifer Heissel and Samuel Norris, "Rise and Shine: The Effect of School Start Times on Academic Performance from Childhood through Puberty," April 13, 2017, https://teensneed sleep.files.wordpress.com/2014/10/heissel-et-al-rise-and-shine -the-effect-of-school-start-times-on-academic-performance-from -childhood-through-puberty.pdf.

7. Richard Obday, *The Healing Sun: Sunlight and Health in the 21st Century* (Rochester, VT: Findhorn, 2000), 11.

8. Scripture differentiates between appropriate "glory" (Greek *doxa*), reserved exclusively for the Most High, and glory misappropriated by humans for themselves. Paul called this *kenodoxia*, or "empty glory" (Galatians 5:26; Philippians 2:3). Among the most damnable acts of mankind recorded in Romans 1 was that of

redirecting God's rightful *doxa* to "images made to look like mortal man and birds and animals and reptiles" (Romans 1:23).

9. Garry Friesen, *Decision Making and the Will of God* (1980: repr., Colorado Springs: Multnomah, 2004), 191, bold original.

10. Friesen, *Decision Making*, 190, italics original.

ABOUT THE AUTHOR

Tom Bennardo has operated in the church planting world for the better part of three decades. His experience spans the spectrum—church planter, sending church lead pastor, church planting mentor and coach, and leader of a church planting network.

Tom is co-director of the Synergy Church Planting Network (www.synergychurchplanting.com), which identifies, trains, and coaches church planters across the United States. He also serves as director of pastoral development and Western US church multiplication for the Fellowship of Evangelical Churches (www .fecministries.org), providing training and theological education tracts for current and emerging pastors.

Tom holds an MDiv from Grace Theological Seminary and a doctorate from Trinity Evangelical Divinity School. He is a sought-after speaker and seminar leader, as well as a consultant in church leadership and organization.

A New York City native, Tom is an avid sports fan who lives and (mostly) dies with the New York Mets and Jets every season and a mediocre athlete whose past accomplishments grow greater in his mind with every passing year.

Tom and his wife, Marcia, have two daughters. He's never surfed but resides in San Clemente, California, for the view.